CURIOSITA TEACHING
INSTRUCTIONAL STRATEGIES

Patti Garrett Shade   Dr. Richard Shade

CLC0490
© 2011 Pieces of Learning
Printing 5 4 3 2
Marion IL
ISBN 978-1-937113-07-0
Printed by
McNaughton & Gunn, Inc
Saline MI
12/2012

curiosita logo by Matt Wallen

Table of Contents

Creativity . . . What Do You Believe?

Indicate your level of agreement with each statement. Use the following scale:

S   **Strong agreement**

A   **Agreement**

D   **Disagreement**

SD   **Strong Disagreement**

___1. The creative students often cause problems in classroom due to their disruptive behaviors.

___2. You can teach a student to think more creatively.

___ 3. Creativity is a rare trait, only found in a few people.

___ 4. I can identify the students in my classroom who are the most creative.

___ 5. A paper-and-pencil test does not really measure a student's creative ability.

___ 6. There aren't any teaching tools that can be used to teach creativity.

___ 7. Teaching with creativity will help students learn and retain core content knowledge.

___ 8. Technology is replacing the need for creative thinkers in the workforce.

___ 9. Creative teaching is one method that can be used to teach diverse learning populations.

___ 10. Businesses are seeking employees who have strong content knowledge because they can teach them to be creative.

___ 11. Critical thinking is part of the creative learning process.

___ 12. It is important to assess creativity.

___ 13. Highly creative learners are part of the diverse learning populations.

___ 14. Creative learning environments distract students from their lessons.

Introduction

Curiosita, "an insatiable curious approach to life and an unrelenting quest for continuous learning - comes first because the desire to know, to learn, and to grow is the powerhouse of knowledge, wisdom, and discovery" (Gelb, 1998, p. 9).

One of the biggest misconceptions about the use of creativity (creative thinking) in schools is that it "belongs" only in the areas of art, music, drama, and dance. It is true that creativity is the mainstay in these classes, but we need it in all content areas. We can use creative thinking to make learning environments, including required core standard materials, more meaningful and engaging for students. Creative thinking is a tool that provides students with interesting and unusual ways to learn, and offers teachers new instructional techniques for designing exciting and engaging standards-based courses or enrichment course offerings. The activities and the accompanying extensions in the *Curiosita Teaching Handbook of Instructional Strategies* move what even we as educators consider the "rote or required" learning from the routine to the enjoyable. You may also see your reluctant students move from uninspired onlookers to absorbed and engaged learners.

Teaching with and for creativity will result in changes or modifications that enhance all areas of instruction and curricular design. However, creative thinking must first be approached as a developmental skill. As in all developmental teaching endeavors, the early stages are devoted to skill building and providing opportunities for practice and application. When students are learning a new skill, whether it is shooting free throws on the basketball court, riding a bike, reading, or learning the parts of grammar, they must practice the skill in order to improve. When they do this, they are not only improving their skill level, but also, perhaps more importantly, their confidence level. As they become more confident and more successful, they feel better prepared to attempt more difficult aspects of that skill.

As you view skill development in the classroom, you might see students moving from journaling and writing essays to authoring and publishing their work! It is the same with the skills of creative thinking. Practice in a supportive and challenging environment leads to incremental and sometimes "big leaps" in creative thinking skill abilities. Teachers observe that students will be seen as "creatively challenged," while others will almost daily Knock-My-Socks-Off (K.M.S.☺.) with their performances.

The integration of creativity into daily lessons offers students pathways for making personally meaningful connections to prior learning. The initial change in daily instruction may begin simply with the introduction of fluency and flexibility exercises. Next, teachers begin the important work of reviewing their lessons and infusing the Elements of Creativity and the components of the Creativity Fan into their instructional and curricular design. Every step of the creativity instructional process places students in idea-generating and/or idea focusing modes. This results in a dynamic learning atmosphere where ideas and concepts are deeply imprinted onto their grey matter. This type of learning environment fosters not only the development of creativity, but also ensures rapid and more enduring mastery of content. *The Curiosita Teaching Handbook of Instructional Strategies* also contains detailed lessons associated with the Creativity Introductory Scope and Sequence (C.I.S.S.) to support a developmental approach to the integration of creativity into the instructional process.

CREATIVITY INTRODUCTORY SCOPE AND SEQUENCE

ALL TEACHERS AT THE BEGINNING OF EVERY YEAR

CLIMATE ACTIVITIES

1. Introductory Activities	That's Me Roles and Responsibilities No Problem Game
2. Learning & Thinking Style Assessments	Multibilities Activities Right & Left Brain Investigations Gender Sort Activity

INDIVIDUAL TEACHER OR TEAM OF TEACHERS

GUIDELINES & PROCESS ACTIVITIES

3. Brainstorming Activities	Brainstorming Dissection I & II Telethink Brainstorming Quiz
4. Elements Activities	Elements Activity
5. Creative & Critical Thinking Activities	Creative & Critical Poems Creative & Critical Test

THINKING TOOLS

6. SCAMPER & REPMACS Activities	SCAMPER & REPMACS Activities & Test
7. Think Tank Activities	Think Tank: Creative Story Writing
8. Critical Thinking Tools	PMQ & Choice Boards

NOTE: Items 3 – 8 may be taught to students by an individual teacher or divided among a team.

ALL TEACHERS THROUGHOUT YEAR

- Integrate the Elements of Creativity and the Thinking Vocabulary into their lesson plans.
- Infuse the Guidelines and Process Activities into instruction and curricular design.
- Design curriculum around product-based learning to provide students with opportunities to create and to encourage the development of all components of the Creativity Fan.
- Put *creativity* on the team agenda and have fun working together to design a program integrated with *creativity*!

> *"We do not grow into creativity, we grow out of it – or rather, we're educated out of it." Sir Kenneth Robinson*

The Handbook of Instructional Strategies includes the following sections:

1. Climate Activities
2. Learning and Thinking Style Assessment Activities
3. Brainstorming Activities
4. Elements of Creativity Activities
5. Creative and Critical Thinking Activities
6. Think Tank Activities
7. Flexibility and Perception Activities
8. Animation: Product-based Learning Unit
9. The Brains: Product-based Learning Unit
10. Passion Learning: Product-based Learning Unit
11. Products & Wiki Resources (On CD only)

1. The **Climate Activities** assist in establishing an environment or atmosphere so creative learning may flourish. It can be described as "setting the stage" for creativity. It involves building relationships with students and structuring the classroom for improved physical, mental, emotional, and social interactions. These help both the student and teacher manage the classroom, as well as the thinking and learning processes, to elicit improved creative output and achievement.

2. The **Learning and Thinking Style Assessment Activities** present suggestions and model lessons for the recognition and acceptance of the diversity of student learning and thinking styles. This is an essential foundation for both students and teachers as they begin the journey to discover how an *increased awareness of these differences* enhances instruction and interactions between students in the creative classroom. One big first step is making students aware of their learning differences through the assessment of their Multiblities, Right and Left Brain Characteristics, and Gender Traits. When students and teachers discover these differences in themselves, it creates both a sense of excitement in the classroom as well as an atmosphere where acceptance of individual learning diversity becomes the norm.

3. The **Brainstorming Activities** include the initial tools and procedures necessary to support a skills-based developmental approach to creativity. These provide not only the original form of Brainstorming (with its associated rules) but also include a variety of Brainstorming techniques: Creative Brainstorming, Pass Arounds, That's Me, Quick Thinks, Tele-think, and Think-Pair-Share. Using these structured forms of Brainstorming *intensifies* and *multiplies* the output of any Brainstorming session.

4. The **Elements of Creativity** activity is designed to introduce students to the four Elements of Creativity. Fluency, Flexibility, Originality, and Elaboration are essential skills for all students in creative classrooms. The four Elements provide teachers with instructional focus as they assess student creative skill development. This section also includes an activity that dispels the numerous myths of creativity that may block or impede the level of student participation or teacher buy-in.

5. The **Creative and Critical Thinking** templates (SCAMPER, PMQ, and Choice Boards) have many, quite possibly unlimited, uses in the creative classroom. Each approach creative or critical thinking processes with some form of a graphic organizer to help students disaggregate their thinking into the most appropriate sections. This process further challenges students to reflect upon and gain a greater understanding of their own thinking.

6. **Think Tanks** can be effectively used in a variety of ways. The simple, basic design of the Think Tank gives teachers leeway to employ a variety of approaches for using this instrument. It also reminds students that this is a class that focuses on *thinking* in a collaborative atmosphere – much like a business Think Tank. These tools challenge students to use focused thinking approaches in order to generate and organize their thoughts. A variety of Think Tanks are included, such as: Creative Story Planner, Innovation Creation, Sensory, and the Think Tank Problem Solving Game.

7. The activities in the **Flexibility and Perception** section are designed to keep the brain engaged, flexible, and agile. Flexibility and perception are two unique skill areas of creative thinking. At first, these areas may seem somewhat nebulous in nature, but once they are introduced and embedded into the curriculum, their value and importance become apparent. Initially, their powerful impact on students' thinking may not be noticed. With continued, purposeful, planned use, teachers will begin to see an incredible change in students' skills in these two areas. Using these tools assists students in "breaking barriers of perception" . . . opening the doorways to the world of creative thoughts and ideas. This leads to enhanced imagination, improved visualization of thought, increased independence in thinking, and an openness to tinkering and playfulness of thought. Exercising the brain is as important as exercising the body!

8. The **Animation Unit** takes students on a tour of the process of animation through the development of a series of products. This unit begins with students learning the terms and processes required for animation to occur. Next they design simple thaumatrope animations to test their skill and understanding. Students then move on to the development of flipbooks and digital animations. The unit culminates with students working in a variety of mediums (coin, chalk, clay, etc.) to produce their final animation. Working on animations may be "just the ticket" that unleashes the full power of student creativity.

9. The **Brain Unit** has the goal of increasing core content knowledge along with developing students' creative outputs. For some students this dual purpose increases engagement and enjoyment of the lessons. This unit demonstrates how high levels of complex content (anatomy and physiology) can be intertwined with creativity to intensify the learning process. For some teachers this experience solidifies their understanding of how creativity can be used to augment all core content instruction.

10. **Passion Learning** provides students with the freedom to explore intense levels of interest along with opportunities for open-ended explorations of their creative abilities – clear avenues for the development of a love of learning!

11. The **Product and Wiki Resource** section gives students and teachers a wide variety of resources to use for developing and publishing creative work products. Today's students need opportunities to create for the sake of creating and opportunities to transform knowledge gained into real life, product-based 21st century learning experiences.

ELEMENTS OF CREATIVITY

The Elements of Creativity provide a structure for infusing creativity into instructional design. Using the Elements during different phases of instruction provides opportunities to elicit student output within each of the four areas:

- **Fluency -** generating a great number of ideas.

- **Flexibility -** creating ideas in a wide range of categories.

- **Originality -** producing unique, novel, or one-of-a-kind ideas.

- **Elaboration -** adding details to enrich, refine, or embellish ideas.

When students are immersed in creative thinking lessons or activities, the Elements are the targeted student outcomes.

THE CREATIVITY FAN

The Creativity Fan provides a model of seven areas that can be developed in students to help them improve or more fully develop their creative abilities. Each area has accompanying student and teacher goals to guide instruction and curricular design.

14

1. PROCESS–thinking patterns, procedures, and pathways.

Student Process Goals:
Attitude: Students will view thinking as a skill that can be improved.
Ability:　Students will demonstrate mastery of new thinking tools and procedures.

Teacher Process Goal:
Teachers will introduce students to a variety of thinking tools, procedures, and processes.

2. PERSISTENCE–effort, diligence, or task commitment.

Student Persistence Goals:
Attitude: Students will view failure as an opportunity to learn.
Ability:　Students will demonstrate the ability to continue to work hard at a task until they achieve success.

Teacher Persistence Goal:
Teachers will mentor students through the cyclic process of success and failure involved in creativity.

3. PRODUCT–verbal or visual demonstrations of learning.

Student Product Goals:
Attitude: Students will view products as the necessary vehicle to demonstrate their creativity.
Ability:　Students will demonstrate creativity through a variety of visual and verbal products.

Teacher Product Goal:
Teachers will provide students with opportunities to create simple and complex visual and verbal products.

4. PERCEPTION–viewpoints or perspectives.

Student Perception Goals
Attitude: Students will internalize "breaking their mental chains" as a way of acquiring new viewpoints and/or perspectives.
Ability:　Students will be able to look at ideas, thoughts, and objects and generate multiple perspectives.

Teacher Perception Goal:
Teachers will schedule daily activities that challenge students to change their perceptions.

5. PASSION–intense desire or love for a concept or idea.

Student Passion Goals:
Attitude: Students will believe that learning can be intense, joyful, and energizing.
Ability: Students will immerse themselves deeply in creative endeavors, losing an awareness of time and other things around them (Flow).

Teacher Passion Goal:
Teachers will plan a wide variety of activities that address student strengths and interests so students can explore and discover passion areas of learning.

6. PERSON–individual traits or behaviors.

Student Person Goals:
Attitude: Students will enjoy everything about creating for its own sake.
Ability: Students will learn and understand how oppositional characteristics contribute to creativity.

Teacher Person Goal:
The teacher will coach students to increase their awareness and appreciation of creative behaviors and traits.

7. PRESS–physical, psychological, or emotional influences.

Student Press Goals:
Attitude: Students will be open to conventional or unconventional means of stimulating creative thinking.
Ability: Students will identify and select forms of the press that increase their personal creative output.

Teacher Press Goal:
The teacher will introduce students to a variety of forms of the press.

The seven components of this model depict the areas of development that can be targeted when students are immersed in a program of creativity and creative thinking.

> *"Inquisitive minds are the safeguards of our democracy, now and forever. But even of greater importance, inquisitive minds are the promise of living enriching lives; they are the energizers of our growing and thriving civilizations." Barell*

Terms, Templates, and Techniques

As you read and work through sections 1-10 of the *Handbook of Instructional Strategies*, you will discover a number of terms, templates, and techniques that occur repeatedly in the lessons and activities. The following section is designed as a glossary to provide you with an overview to peruse as you select activities to use in your classroom.

1. Anchoring Activity is an on-going activity or activities that students can go to at any point during instruction to keep them actively engaged in the learning process. It can be used for students who finish early or to create time for a teacher to work with individuals and small groups.

2. Brainstorming is a tool for generating options. It involves a deliberate search for a large number of possibilities to address or deal with tasks or ideas. These are challenges that require new possibilities and/or different perspectives of one or more individuals. This tool focuses on producing a variety of options that are unique and novel. Brainstorming is founded on the principal of deferred judgment in order for all ideas to be elicited freely. It is much different from everyday conversations, debates, or lectures in its purpose and outcome.

Brainstorming is most often used in a group setting but can be successfully used by an individual. Brainstorming sessions are often guided by a facilitator or experienced group leader but are also found to be useful for novice individual thinkers. Brainstorming is a powerful tool that creates synergy and leverage of the combined perspectives of all members of a group. It is a problem solving and/or idea generation method that uses creative group thinking to generate bold and innovative ideas (Adapted from Center for Creative Learning, Inc., 1998).

3. Brainstorming Rules 1) Many Ideas 2) Piggyback 3) Free-Wheel 4) Defer Judgment.

4. Call-backs is a process using recall; you ask students to revisit previously learned information. Call-backs challenge students to reflect upon a concept formerly taught in connection with new instruction.

5. Card Sort is a process that challenges students to put statement cards in arrangements that show groupings or true-false categories.

6. Creative Thinking is a mental and social process involving the generation of new ideas, connections, or meanings between existing concepts. It is an assumption-breaking process that occurs through encountering gaps, paradoxes, opportunities, challenges, or concerns and then searching for meaningful new connections by using **divergent** thinking for **generating**:

- Many possibilities,
- Varied possibilities,
- Possibilities from different perspectives,
- Unusual or original possibilities, and
- Details to expand or enrich possibilities.

(Adapted from Center for Creative Learning, Inc., 1998)

7. Critical Thinking is a mental process of discernment, analysis, and evaluation. It involves reflecting upon an idea, decision, or task with solid, common sense judgment, examining possibilities carefully, fairly, and constructively, and then **focusing** you thoughts and actions by using **convergent** thinking for:

- Organizing and analyzing
- Synthesizing and reconstructing
- Refining and developing promising possibilities
- Reviewing with relevance and logic
- Ranking or prioritizing options
- Choosing or deciding on certain options

(Adapted from Center for Creative Learning, Inc., 1998)

8. Force Fit is a tool that assists students in brainstorming. The process involves looking at the attributes of two seemingly unrelated items to generate new and unusual ideas or concepts.

9. K.M.S.☺. is the awarding of an extra five points for any creative product that is judged to be incredibly outstanding.

10. Mini-Conferences are short formal or informal discussion sessions between a teacher and a student or group of students. These formative assessment conferences are primarily for the purpose of discussing areas of improvement and setting the goal for the next level of creative productivity.

11. Peer Review occurs as students continually work on creative products and have fellow students formatively assess their work. This guides the development of their products and serves as a reminder of the continuous improvement process necessary for creative productivity.

12. PMQ is a three column graphic organizer that helps students categorize their thinking into the pluses, minuses, and questions they have about an idea or process.

13. Questioning in the creative classroom is for the purpose of expanding ideas and products. This type of questioning usually involves open-ended prompts from the teacher to stimulate student thinking.

14. Quick Writes start when a teacher gives a prompt for students to write to or brainstorm a list within a short time frame.

15. R.E.D.☺. is an assessment of the current status of a product and it cues students that they have an opportunity to keep working to obtain an acceptable level of achievement or even a K.M.S.☺. level of achievement.

16. Rubrics are assessment grids that guide the development and evaluation of student work products.

17. SCAMPER is a checklist tool that stimulates students thinking processes within seven categories of thought: Substitute, Combine, Adapt, Magnify/Minify, Put To Other Uses, Eliminate, and Reverse/Rearrange.

18. Slapstick Review begins by dividing students into two teams. The teacher posts a selection of answers or "True and False" on a flip chart that is on a stand. When the teacher reads a statement or question one student from each team runs to the board and slaps the correct answer with a spatula.

19. **Tele-think** is a brainstorming process. It begins with students lining up around the room and passing (whispering) a brainstormed word from one student to another. The ideas are then shared out loud for the group to enjoy and reflect upon the creativity of the answers. Students are encouraged to focus on the attributes of the word to come up with unusual connections.

20. Temperature Feedback is used to guide student thinking in a supportive way by evaluating their ideas or answers as Cold, Cool, Warm, Warmer, or Hot.

21. That's Me is a flexible activity that emphasizes student difference in opinions, interests, ideas, thoughts, etc. Teachers or students make statements and the other students stand up and shout "That's Me" if the statement describes them or they agree with the statement. It can also be used academically as a pre-assessment or formative assessment process.

22. **Think Tanks** are graphic organizers that can be designed for multiple purposes inside and outside of content areas to help stimulate and organize student thinking.

23. Think-Pair-Share is a process where students are challenged first to think individually, then with a partner, and then with the whole group.

24. Tic-Tac-Toe is a teacher and/or student designed choice board for the selection of product(s) a student will complete for a particular unit of study.

25. Trial and Error is the strategy of trying over and over while purposefully adjusting each attempt with a new twist or idea to generate an improvement in the outcome or final product. This simple process reminds students that "failure" is a learning opportunity!

Alvin Toffler . . .

"The illiterate of the twenty-first century will not be those who cannot read or write, but those who cannot learn, unlearn, and relearn." We need students who can think!

"Brain" Thinking Vocabulary

1. **BRAIN CHART** - Individuals or teams submit their favorite or best responses from a written brainstormed list of ideas. The teacher records verbally submitted answers on a flipchart, whiteboard, or graphic organizer for group or whole class review.

2. **BRAIN DUMP** - Students quickly generate and record ideas or words and then cross them out or throw them away. Then students are asked to repeat the same brainstorming task to generate new and different answers.

3. **BRAIN ONLY** - When students hear this announced, *"move to a your 'brain only' spot"* at the beginning of an activity, it alerts them to move anywhere in the classroom they are comfortable and away from any other student. This also indicates students cannot ask questions of the teacher or other students during this time.

4. **BRAIN PASS** - An object is passed around the room to stimulate the generation of ideas in a brainstorming session.

5. **BRAIN POST** - Students post ideas quickly and randomly on flip charts or a blank wall using Post-its® or index cards. This can be done individually or as a group.

6. **BRAIN SET** - This is when the teacher sets-up or prepares students for the learning processes that are going to occur. This often involves using combinations of different stimuli (forms of the Press) such as timing, music, lighting, location, movement, or visual images to create the mood or atmosphere for the proposed task.

7. **BRAIN SHARE** - Teachers quickly go around the room soliciting a response from each individual (usually sequentially) in the class after an initial incubation and brainstorming period. This can be done separately or as part of the Think-Pair-Share activity.

8. **BRAIN STARTER** - This is an activity given to students at the beginning of a class or lesson to set them up for the activity to follow. It may also be used to work on the development of one or more of the Elements of Creativity.

9. **BRAIN VOTE** - After organizing or grouping a set of brainstormed solutions or ideas, students are asked to "spend" (place) three colored sticky dots on their favorite choices.

10. **BRAIN WALK** - Students walk from table to table on the teacher's cue, rotating clockwise or counterclockwise, to add ideas, to evaluate products, or to get ideas from items, objects, or other student's products.

11. BRAIN WASTING - This statement signals to students they are "wasting brain cells" with the comment or question they just made. When students get this response (with a touch of humor) it reminds them that they need to get back on task and/or do a better job of listening to instructions.

12. BRAIN WRITE - Students are instructed to write one idea on a paper according to the stated task. Next they put the paper back in the middle of the table and select a different paper to add another idea onto the list. A Brain Walk can be added towards the end of the task so that students move from table to table in an effort to generate more ideas (piggyback) on other groups' papers.

The activities created for the *Handbook of Instructional Strategies* have been carefully designed to challenge different mental abilities and attitudes of students. Educators are encouraged to *script-teach* the lessons as written the first time they teach them to students. The comments, questions, and timing of events have been very purposefully positioned in each lesson. They have been carefully planned, refined, and improved upon over years of teaching. These meticulous prompts and directions are coordinated to produce the maximum engagement and growth for students involved in the learning processes. Teacher adjustments and personalization of activities are later encouraged as the teacher reflects on each lesson taught and then scripts new adaptations or versions. Educators are encouraged to explore, expand, adapt, and modify these activities to fit their personal teaching style and/or content area of instruction. The art of teaching with creativity and creative thinking is a never-ending exercise in "How can it get better?" When making instructional adjustments, it is useful to announce and/or discuss these ideas for change with students to further model the process of cyclic improvement of work - both the "teacher work" and the "student work."

Finally, we would encourage you to start (with a discerning eye) to collect creative additional activities and lessons that support your instructional goals. Why the caveat of "a discerning eye?" There is a big difference between selecting thinking activities that align with content and purpose of instruction and selecting those that appear to be creative, but involve little or no thinking. These latter types of activities do little to improve instruction, take up valuable time, and in some cases, put creativity in a poor limelight. An example of such an activity would be word searches - there is very little thinking or creativity involved.

The world is constantly changing, and with those ever-present changes come new problems and situations requiring new ways of thinking and accompanying new ways of teaching and learning. Creativity is the impetus required to spark ideas and the risk-taking necessary for us to continue living in a productive and progressive world. Our modern society is increasingly dependent on creativity and innovation to grow and prosper. Edward de Bono states, "As competition intensifies, so does the need for creative thinking. It is no longer enough to do the same thing better. It is no longer enough to be efficient and to solve problems. Far more is needed." Creativity, once infused, will forever change teaching styles with lessons based upon collaborative experiences; powerful learning derived from what students say, what they do, and most importantly, what they produce. Learning to think is not passive; it is active and engaging. Watch your students become a community of creative thinkers!

As you examine and explore the creative thinking processes you will discover their relationship to all students' learning. New insights into their impact on the teaching and learning environment begin to emerge. Perhaps, these can best be captured by a student in this statement:

> "As I look at my life today, the things that I value about myself, my imagination, my love of acting, my passion for writing, my love of learning, my curiosity, came from the way that I was parented and taught. And none of these qualities that I just mentioned, none of these qualities that I prize so deeply, none of these qualities that have brought me so much joy, that have made me so successful professionally, none of these qualities that make me who I am can be tested."

-Matt Damon, 2011

Life

Do more than exist, live.
Do more than touch, feel.
Do more than look, observe.
Do more than read, absorb.
Do more than hear, listen.
Do more than think, ponder.
and
Do more . . . create!

- John H. Rhoades (modified)

Curiosita Teaching: Author's Interview: Q & A

1. What is creativity?

We like to say that creativity begins with an attitude! It is being open to ideas, possibilities, and having a mindset of continuous improvement. In the classroom it's about creating passion learning environments. An example is when students look up and say, "Class can't be over yet." This signals they are so deeply immersed in their work they lose track of time and their surroundings. This level of involvement is described by Csikszentmihalyi (1990) as being in Flow. He did case studies of famous creative individuals and found they all describe having this type of experience.

2. Can creativity be taught?

Definitely! Any student can improve his or her creative thinking by learning tools, tips, and techniques. It's practicing that improves self-confidence leading to greater risk-taking – essential for creativity. Practice in creativity involves a cyclic process of success and failure. The repetition of "trying and tweaking" in product development allows students to get over their fear of looking foolish (FOLF)! Creativity is a skill that can be taught, but just like other skills, some people have a predisposition for being highly creative.

3. How does teaching creativity support real world needs?

Our world is where it is because of creative thinkers. What our world becomes will be because of creative thinkers. The biggest change is that almost any job in the work force today requires creative thinking and creative problem solving. Technology has leveled the playing field for most businesses – they are now aggressively searching for creative employees. Take a look at the classified section of the newspapers. Employers are seeking applicants who are creative, self-motivated, innovative, bring new ideas, have a passion for success, etc. These are the essential skill sets of the 21st century workforce.

4. What is the need for creativity in schools?

In the past, the answers were often "in the back of the book." When our kids leave school today we don't even know what the questions are. We need to teach them to be skilled thinkers inside and outside of the box. Students have also lost many opportunities to be joyously and intensely engaged in learning. Many things that are important to developing life-long learners have been erased from the classroom. There is a long list of entrepreneurial world leaders who dropped out of our schools. Creativity in the classroom brings it all back, the important and valid reasons why individuals chose to become teachers.

5. What is the Curiosita Teaching Program™ (CTP™)?

The Curiosita Teaching Program™ pulls together all of the necessary ingredients of creativity and infuses them into all areas of teaching and learning. We started with a philosophy, rationale, and research and developed them into concrete instructional tools and templates that can be used for curricular design. We created pieces for the climate, assessment, and all the necessary instructional tools - in other words, the whole package – so teachers can pick it up and run with it. Maybe, more importantly, they feel that they have permission to teach with creativity. CTP™ is built on teaching in a learning environment where standards and creativity can co-exist and merge seamlessly.

6. What is the philosophy of the CTP™?

It's built around looking backwards at what worked for us as learners and what we saw in our class-rooms when our students expressed a love for learning and were also producing at high levels. We connected this with some of the major initiatives that had changed our teaching practice and developed the philosophy for the program. We call it the Multibilities philosophy. It merges the love or passion for learning with practical, emotional, creative, and diverse learning skills.

7. What are the Elements of Creativity?

It's impossible to remember all the definitions of creativity, as there are over 100! We focused on four of the Elements that are part of many definitions: Fluency, Flexibility, Elaboration, and Original-ity. In CTP™ we define the Elements as developmental skills. This gives teachers an instructional fo-cus. They see their role as guiding the development of the Elements in all students. The Elements be-come "routine" or intertwined in daily instruction. Traditionally the Elements have been used as as-sessments to identify creative thinkers. We are reversing the purpose by teaching them to all stu-dents to use as part of their thinking toolbox.

8. What is the Creativity Fan?

The seven components of the Creative Fan model depict areas that can be further developed in all students to increase their creative productivity. Each component has accompanying student and teacher goals to make them a more definitive part of the creative teaching process. To carry the analogy a bit further, we describe creativity as "turning on the fan!" Two of our favorite "fan blades" are passion and persistence, as these are ones that can be inspirational and drive students to create K.M.S.☺. products!

9. How do the Rules of Brainstorming affect the learning environment?

Brainstorming can be a powerful thinking process, but often we find that it is used informally or "just for fun" in the classroom. When it is used in this way it can actually block or impede students' think-ing. How do you react when someone says, "Go brainstorm"? It is important that the four rules be observed: Many Ideas, Freewheel, Piggyback, and Defer Judgment. These rules say to students, "All ideas are accepted. I can be wild and crazy. I can add on to other students' thoughts, and no one is going to judge me during the brainstorming process." We take the Brainstorming process a step fur-ther in our program by saying it not OK to tell students to "Go brainstorm." Teachers must give them a tool or strategy to increase the impact of Brainstorming and for students to view it as a respectable learning process.

10. What conditions are necessary for the creative classroom climate?

The creative classroom is best described as flexible and open to diverse ideas and opinions. It is a safe environment where students can go a little wild with their thoughts and ideas. It definitely is a place where students can discuss and/or argue on a meta-cognitive level. Students have the freedom *to think about thinking* and are challenged to bring their thoughts to fruition through creative prod-ucts that can be viewed and enjoyed by all. It is also a classroom where structure and organization are in place as essential supports for the creative classroom.

11. How do the characteristics of creative students affect the classroom?

Highly creative students bring all of their oppositional traits to the classroom. By oppositional we are not talking about students being difficult or stubborn, but we are referring to the complexity of the traits creative students exhibit. Instead of having a personality, Csikszentmihalyi (1996) refers to the creative personality as a *multitude*. These traits, when expressed, can stimulate the learning atmosphere of the classroom and at the same time inhibit some students' expressions of their thinking or sometimes isolate the creative learner. In *Curiosita Teaching – Integrating Creative Thinking Into Your 21st Century Classroom* we created an instrument for teachers to use to more purposefully acknowledge and understand the traits of highly creative students. It is called the Creative Attribute Learning Log (C.A.L.L.). Teachers use this daily log to track creative learning traits of their students.

12. How does questioning change in the creative classroom?

In the creative classroom questioning takes on a new role in that it is used to provoke students into expressing themselves more and more creatively. Teachers will use question stems, such as, how might we, what if, how else, etc., to push student thinking outside of the box. When students are in pre-school they ask about 100 questions a day. Beginning in late elementary students stop asking so many questions. In the creative classroom, a data point teachers need to focus on is "how many questions did my students ask today?"

13. Why is product-based-learning an essential part of the creative classroom?

Product-based learning provides both the time and the requirement of a creative output that students need to hone their creative skills. **Creating** is now recognized as the highest level of thinking in the newly revised Bloom's Taxonomy. In our classrooms we must provide opportunities for our students to use knowledge gained to create. Most of our students will live and work in a world where they will be asked to create. Technology today has taken over many of the mundane skills that were once required of a large segment of our workforce. Those jobs no longer exist; we are rapidly moving into an age that will be led by entrepreneurial creative thinkers.

14. Why is it important to assess creativity?

Assessment also takes on a new role in the creative classroom. The primary purpose is for the formative evaluation of creative products. This builds a new relationship among students and teachers, as "we are in this together – let's see how good we can make it together." It still is clearly communicated to the student that the teacher is a mentor, coach, or trainer who guides their learning. Yet, sometimes in the creative classroom the teacher becomes the student as they try to understand and value the creative outputs of their students – creativity has no boundaries. If creativity is not assessed, it will not be recognized as a powerful learning tool. In these instances it will remain as something we do for fun and not necessarily for learning.

15. How does teaching with and for creativity meet the needs of our diverse learners?

Highly creative individuals can now be recognized as one of the diverse learning populations. Their thinking often does not fit with the norm, nor is it easily understood or appreciated by their peers and teachers. Exploring creativity as part of all learning opens new doors for all diverse populations. Some students in these populations do not have the skill sets to express their high levels of thinking in words or written communication. Creativity has a strong visual-spatial component that somewhat levels the playing field for these learners. Adding creativity to the learning process is a new tool that supports the acceptance and understanding of diverse learners.

References

Csikszentmihalyi, M. (1990). Flow: The psychology of optimal experience. New York, NY: Harper & Row, Publishers Inc.

Csikszentmihalyi, M. (1996). Creativity: Flow and the psychology of discovery and invention. New York, NY: HarperCollins, Publishers, Inc. (p. 57).

Fantastic Finds

BOOKS

- Eberle, B. (1996). *Scamper: Creative Games and Activities for Imagination Development.* ISBN: 1-882664-24-8.
- Eberle, B. (1996). *Scamper On: More Creative Games and Activities for Imagination Development.* ISBN: 1-882664-25-6.
  In 1953, Alex Osborn created a list of words and phrases that led to "Idea Spurring Questions" designed to assist participants with the practice of brainstorming. In 1981, Bob Eberle organized those words, phrases, and questions into the acronym SCAMPER. These activity books allow students to develop their imaginations and creativity skills through a series of guided activities.

- Osborn, A. (1953/1993). *Applied Imagination: Principles and Procedures of Creative Problem-Solving.* ISBN: 0-930222-933.
  Alex Osborn was a partner in the world's largest advertising agency, and in the 1940s and 50s wanted to encourage his employees to be more creative and forthright with their ideas. Hence, he created the process known as brainstorming. This book is his best known work and includes numerous topics to explore, activities, and references.

WEBSITES

- http://www.odysseyofthemind.com/ - Odyssey of the Mind
  "*Odyssey of the Mind* is an international educational program that provides creative problem-solving opportunities for students from kindergarten through college. Team members apply their creativity to solve problems that range from building mechanical devices to presenting their own interpretation of literary classics."

- http://www.idodi.org/ - Destination Imagination
  "Destination ImagiNation allows participants of all ages to access their creativity, learn problem-solving skills, and experience successful teamwork strategies as they develop unique solutions to Challenges. By working together to develop solutions, participants push the limits of their imaginations to better themselves and best their competition."

- http://soinc.org/ - Science Olympiad
  "Science Olympiad is a national non-profit organization dedicated to improving the quality of K-12 science education, increasing male, female and minority interest in science, creating a technologically-literate workforce and providing recognition for outstanding achievement by both students and teachers." One of its major goals is to create a passion for learning science by changing the way sci-

ence is perceived and the way it is taught (with an emphasis on problem solving and hands-on, minds-on constructivist learning practices).

- http://www.inventamerica.org/ - Invent America
"The Invent America! Program provides K-8 students opportunities to learn critical and creative thinking skills through the process of inventing. It integrates the curriculum, helps students synthesize knowledge, and provides hands-on experience in the scientific process."

- http://www.bestinc.org/MVC/ - BEST Robotics
"BEST is a non-profit, volunteer-based organization whose mission is to inspire students to pursue careers in engineering, science, and technology through participation in a sports-like, science and engineering-based robotics competition. There is _no fee_ for schools to compete in BEST."

- http://www.fpspi.org/ - Future Problem Solving
"The Future Problem Solving Program International (FPSPI) engages students in creative problem solving. Founded by creativity pioneer, Dr. E. Paul Torrance, FPSPI stimulates critical and creative thinking skills and encourages students to develop a vision for the future."

- http://www.invent.org/camp/ - Camp Invention
Camp Invention is "a weeklong summer enrichment day experience for children entering grades one through six. The Camp Invention program instills creative problem-solving and critical-thinking skills that will encourage children's future success. Nothing could be more important than investing in your children today for the betterment of their tomorrow."

- http://www.nationalroboticschallenge.org/ - National Robotics Challenge
"At the National Robotics Challenge we believe that engineering is not just about taking the same parts as someone else and changing how they are put together. Engineering is about finding the materials and equipment that is best for the problem you are given." Grades 6-College

"It is now a known fact that nearly all of us can become more creative, if we will. And this very fact may well be the hope of the world. By becoming more creative we can lead brighter lives, and can live better with each other. By becoming more creative we can provide better goods and services to each other, to the result of a higher and higher standard of living. By becoming more creative we may even find a way to bring permanent peace to all the world." - Alex Osborn

I Climate Activity 1

Activity:	Job Board: Roles and Responsibilities
Objective:	1. Students will begin to work collaboratively and responsibly in the classroom. 2. Students will generate creative job titles.
Strategies:	Think-Pair-Share, Brainstorming
Elements:	Fluency, Originality
Fan:	Press, Process
CD:	none

Directions: ....

1. Using a Think-Pair Share (*Process*), have students do a quick write for 60 seconds (*Press*). Students individually jot down (*Brainstorm*) all the tasks that need to be done to keep the classroom functioning. The goal is five or more items. Timing students is one form of *Press*.

2. After 60 seconds ask for a show of hands and check to see how many students came up with five or more tasks (*Fluency*). Now tell students to get a partner (*Pair*) and think for 90 more seconds to see if they can get 10 or more items on their list.

3. Ask for a quick show of hands to see which team(s) wrote 10 or more items on their list (*Fluency*). Ask students to circle the item on their lists they think no one else might have (*Originality*). Now tell students they are going to go quickly around the room and (*Share*) the one they circled. Tell them to mark the task off their list if it is called out by another student and to circle another one to share. Keep going until all lists are exhausted. Recognize student answers (*Originality*) when one or only a few have the same tasks listed.

4. Now have students think under another simple version of the Press. Tell them you are going to give them directions/verbal prompts to challenge their thinking. You will read from the following list of statements to prompt students to come up with new tasks. Give students approximately 30 seconds for each attempt to see if they can add tasks to their lists.

- Look towards the right side of the room (e.g. windows need opened/closed, counters need cleaning, computers need to be started and shut down).
- Look up (e.g. lights, ceiling fans, computer projector).
- Think of the beginning of class (e.g. attendance, pass out supplies, papers).
- Look towards the left side of the room (e.g. supply areas, doors, lights).
- Think of the fire drill ringing (line-leader, emergency attendance roster).
- Look towards the front right corner of the room (game shelves, dictionaries, sink).
- Think outside the classroom (bulletin board, messenger).

5. Now call on students to see if they can add to the task list the ideas they just generated under the Press of both time and verbal prompts.

Note: As the job/task titles are confirmed, the teacher writes the accepted job on an index card or sticky note and puts it in a box. The teacher puts in extras (if needed) for the tasks of passing out and collecting papers so there are enough tasks for each student. Depending on class size, some students may have more than one task.

6. Each student draws a task from the box. Quickly go around the room and have each student state the job they drew. Now have them hold up their hand if they would like to negotiate with another student to trade jobs. Explain to students that jobs will be redrawn each quarter. Post the jobs prominently in the room. You may have students create their own name plates on stock board and decoratively display them in the room. Encourage students to have fun with "awarding their titles" – e.g. Chairperson of Supply!

Reflection: ....

I spend the first two weeks of school getting to know my students and beginning the relationship-building process. I also use this time to introduce some of the simple thinking tools and processes in a fun and relaxed manner. I have used the "Job Board" activity with students from grades K-8, and they all love it and get very protective of their jobs/responsibilities. Very seldom do I get the comment from a student saying they don't want a job. If this happens I respond with, "We are all part of a team, and we all do our part to make the classroom run smoothly and efficiently," or I might also simply state, "That is not one of the choices." It quickly becomes a "norm" of the classroom.

Extension: ....

This could be adapted to discuss the roles and responsibilities different family members have both at home and in their jobs. This could become a growing bulletin board to display tasks as they are discovered over a period of time in conversations with family members.

NOTES

> *"Traditional thinking is all about what is.*
> *Future thinking will also need to be about what can be." de Bono*

I Climate Activity 2

Activity:	**That's Me – Getting to Know You**
Objectives:	Students will appreciate the wide diversity of interests and abilities of other students.
Strategies:	Brainstorm, Quick Write, That's Me
Elements:	Fluency, Flexibility, Originality
Fan:	Person, Press, Perception
CD:	**Climate 2a** That's Me: Student Creativity Questions CD ONLY **Climate 2b** That's Me: Teacher Questions CD ONLY

Directions: ....

1. Tell students you are going to ask them some questions so they can get to know each other better and you can learn more about them (*Person*). Tell them to stand up and say "That's me!" if the statement you read describes them. Read a statement from the student question list below:

1. Who has more than 2 siblings?
2. Who rides the bus to school? Walks?
3. Who likes vegetables?
4. Who has traveled to another state? Country?
5. Who knows how to roller skate? Roller blade?
6. Who has gone skiing?
7. Who can write words backwards?
8. Who knows all the state capitals?
9. Who has a birthday before July? After July?
10. Who can type really, really fast?

2. Next ask students to do a Quick Write and to formulate other interesting, fun, and original questions they would like to ask the class. Give students 90 seconds (*Press*) to write five or more (*Brainstorm*). Tell students to circle the one they think no one else is going to ask (*Originality*). Continue the "That's Me" activity having students ask the questions.

3. Finally, ask the students to do a Quick Write to formulate questions they would like to ask you to get to know you better. Give students 90 seconds to write five or more questions (*Brainstorm*). Ask students (show of hands) "How many had 5 questions? 10 questions? More than 10?" to reinforce the understanding of the element of *Fluency*. Now have students do a Question and Answer session asking you their favorite questions. You can have students raise their hands if the question asked is also on their list helping to build a climate of camaraderie. Recognize students who have original questions to reinforce the Element of Originality after the completion of the question and answer session so you do not inhibit the production of student questions.

Reflection: ....

This is one type of activity that will help you create the atmosphere of recognizing and appreciating the different characteristics, interests, and learning styles of your students. This informal activity is fun for students and gives the teacher new insights. Encourage the students to ask questions that are not related to school that can be answered with a Yes (That's Me = standing up) or a No (That's Not Me = remaining seated).

Extensions: ....

1. The *That's Me: Student Creativity Questions* has been designed around the interests and activities of your students. You can design a variety of formats relating to other student characteristics. For example: a healthy lifestyle list, a self esteem list, a study habits list, etc. This activity is a fun way to reinforce a variety of concepts you want to promote in your classroom.

2. *That's Me: Teacher Questions* **(CD Climate 2b)** can be used for getting to know the staff.

3. *That's Me* Question Sheets can also be designed as pre-assessment and/or post assessments of units of study.

4. Creative Journal Prompts

Creative journal writing is another way for students to share their strengths or interests. The following creative journal prompts may yield more in-depth and "fun" personal insights (*Perception*):

Which are you more like?

The country or the city?	A rock band or an orchestra?
The present or the future?	A rollerblade or a pogo stick?
A turtle or a rabbit?	A river or a lake?
Leather or suede?	A screened-in porch or a bay window?
A computer or a pen?	A mountain or a valley?

You can also use student-generated journal prompts. Collect ideas and draw daily from a box of student suggestions.

5. *That's Me: Student Creativity Questions* **(CD Climate 2a)** is to use with older students when you delve more deeply into discussions of creative characteristics.

NOTE: All the statements with the © at the end are characteristics of creativity.

It is suggested you use the more informal *That's Me Student Questions* (for all ages) as the getting to know you activity.

I Climate Activity 3

Activity:	**No Problem**
Objectives:	Students will use creative and critical thinking to process an understanding of the one classroom rule.
Strategies:	Brainstorming, Think-Pair-Share, Temperature Feedback
Elements:	Flexibility, Originality, Fluency
Fan:	Process, Perception, Press
CD:	**Climate 3a** Think Tank: No Problem Board **Climate 3b** Think Tank: No Problem Board - Student Sample CD ONLY **Climate 3c** Creative Problem Solving Card

Directions: ....

1. Start with an open discussion of classroom rules. Pose the following question to students, "If a teacher has one rule that covers anything in the classroom, what might that rule be?" Process the student thinking by using a Think-Pair-Share (*Process*). Give students 90 seconds (*Press*) to list their ideas (*Brainstorm*) for the one rule of your classroom (*Think*).

2. Call time and ask students to get a partner (*Pair*) and test their "one rule" statements to see if the partners can evaluate their rules to see if it would stop any type of misbehavior in the classroom.

3. Now ask students to *Share* the one they think would stop all problems in the classroom. As students share, ask the group if they could follow the stated rule and still cause a problem. If a student's answer has already been used they may pass in the sharing when it is their turn.

4. This is also a good time to use Temperature Feedback with you students. When they give an answer you would respond with hot, warm, cool, etc. indicating how close they were to the answer. Finally, identify your rule as "Don't cause a problem."

5. Ask the students if they know most everything that causes problems. Most likely they will laugh and tell you some of them are really good at causing problems.

6. Handout the *Problem Solving Card* **(CD Climate 3c)** and go over the process of how using this is intended to have them solve their own problems, understand the impact of their problems, and come up with solutions (sometimes very creative) to keep the problem from reoccurring. Show students a sample Card: **Climate 3b** *Think Tank: No Problem Board-Student Sample.*

7. Now students will play the No Problem Game. Give students the *No Problem Think Tank* handout **(CD Climate 3a)** with the following column labels: PHYSICAL, VISUAL, VERBAL, SOCIAL, and MENTAL (*Flexibility*). The rows are numbered: 1, 2, 3, 4, 5. Next group students into tables of 4 or 5. Ask students for an example of a problem a student might cause within each of the column categories.

PHYSICAL - a problem that involves mostly movement (hitting)

VISUAL - a problem that you mostly observe (making silly faces)

VERBAL - a problem that you hear (using inappropriate language)

SOCIAL - a problem involving groups doing or not doing things together (ignoring one or more students)

MENTAL - a problem caused by thinking or not thinking activity (not paying attention)

8. Explain to students that the problem they identify may fit into one or more categories (*Perception*) but they must choose which category they believe it fits into the best. Now solicit examples of problems from the group that would fit into each of the categories. Discuss what makes them fit. Now tell the teams the challenge is to find a very creative description of the problem using only 1-3 words in each box. Give the teams of 4-5 students time, about 30 minutes, to complete the No Problem Think Tank. Remind them not to let the other teams hear their creative answers.

9. Play the "No Problem Game"

a. The teacher calls out column and row combinations (e.g. Physical #1) and asks each table group to state their creative answer in that box.

b. Points are awarded on the following basis and are recorded in the triangle of each square.

0 points = if two or more teams have the exact answer in the same location

5 points = if each team has a different answer

10 points = if the teacher recognizes the answer as a very creative Knock My Socks Off (K.M.S.☺.) answer (*Originality*). This is at the teacher's total discretion. This is explained to the students in the following manner: The teacher is the referee and no one argues with the referee!

Reflection: ....

This is an activity that allows you to both infuse the elements of creativity into your classroom and establish a fun yet firm management plan with your students. This is an essential ingredient of a creative thinking classroom. It is also establishes a climate of respect between the teacher and the students.

Extensions: ....

1. There are several content activities in the *Think Tank* section of this handbook.

2. The Creative Problem Solving Card can be used anytime a student causes a problem that needs a thinking solution. It is a very effective tool for helping students understand what problem their action or in action actually caused. For example, many students are sometimes tardy, and they might think the problem caused is being tardy. I ask them to think about the real problems the tardy causes, e.g. teacher starting class over or repeating directions. You can also start a running log (like a sign-in sheet) of completed Creative Problem Solving Cards. These cards become very useful pieces of data if the problem escalates or the administration needs to become involved at some point.

3a

Name_____   Date_____

Think Tank: No Problem Board

	PHYSICAL	VERBAL	VISUAL	SOCIAL	MENTAL
1					
2					
3					
4					
5					

3c

Creative Problem Solving Card (CPSC)

"Be part of the solution not part of the problem"

Dear Mom or Dad,

I caused a problem in class today.

Here's my **detailed** description of the problem and why it causes a problem. I . . .

_____

_____

_____

_____

My **specific** plan for solving the problem is to . . .

_____

_____

_____

_____

My teacher has requested I communicate this to you by:

_____ **Phone**   _____**E-mail**   _____**Signed PSC**   _____**Conversation**

_____   _____

Student Signature   Date   Parent Signature   Date

Dear Parents:

This copy of the "Creative Problem Solving Card" is being sent to you to let you know that your son or daughter is working on solving a problem. Please encourage them to discuss their solution choices with you and to keep you posted on how it is working for them. A signed copy of this card is your son or daughter's **pass back into full class participation**.

Sincerely,

_____

Dear Students:

Complete the list below before leaving class today and record your name on the Creative Problem Solving Log sheet.

_____ I've completed a Problem Solving Card for my teacher's file only at this time.

_____ I've completed a Problem Solving Card for my parent(s). I'm taking it home to be signed.

This is my first _____, second_____, or third_____ Other #_____ CPSC

I Climate Activity 4

Activity:	**Student and Teacher Brains**
Objectives:	Students will use creative thinking, critical thinking, and humor to visually portray the "brains" (characteristics) of themselves and their teachers.
Strategies:	Brainstorming, Force Fit
Elements:	Fluency, Flexibility, Originality, and Elabloration
Fan:	Person, Process, Product, Perception, Passion
CD:	**Climate 4a** Alpha Think Tank Handout
	Climate 4b Alpha Think Tank: Name Sample CD ONLY
	Climate 4c Right Brain Template CD ONLY
	Climate 4d Left Brain Template CD ONLY
	Climate 4e1 Student Brain - 1 CD ONLY
	Climate 4e2 Student Brain - 2 CD ONLY
	Climate 4f1 Shade Sample CD ONLY
	Climate 4f2 Shade Sample CD ONLY
	Climate 4f3 Teacher Brain CD ONLY

Directions: ....

1. Students will list (*Brainstorm*) characteristics of themselves and their favorite teacher using a double-sided *Alpha Think Tank Handout* **(CD Climate 4a).** To complete the Alpha Think Tank, students may use one or two-word phrases that begin with each letter of the alphabet (*Force Fit*) to list a characteristic of themselves and their teachers. Encourage students to focus on coming up with creative unusual ways (*Flexibility/Originality*) to describe the characteristic. Challenge students to Force Fit their first and last names into the first row and column of the *Alpha Think Tank* **(CD Climate 4b).** The sample using Patti Shade fits, but many student names will not. This is a fun and creative way for each student to come up with a "new version" of their names.

2. Once the *Alpha Think Tanks* have been generated (*Process*), students us a *blank brain template* **(CD Climate 4c, 4d - use right or left)** to determine the proportions of the brain that will be allotted for each of the characteristics (*Perception*). For example, it may be funny to have a large area for *sports* and a very small area for *homework*. Exaggeration is an incredibly effective technique that combines creativity and humor. Students do not have to put all of the characteristics from the Think Tanks on the brains. They may also choose to combine some of the characteristics into more interesting descriptions.

3. Students will complete draft brain templates of themselves and of their favorite teacher. Remind them to use exaggeration and have fun with the proportions they allot for each characteristic. Students should first pencil-draft the proportions and contents and then, after a mini-conference with the teacher, work further to add details (*Elaboration* and *Originality)* to the final product. Students will find it useful to get ideas and feedback from their peers during this process.

4. Students may also use symbols and drawings to represent the characteristics on the completed brains (*Product*).

Reflection: ....

1. This activity requires conversation and feedback between students and the teacher to create (*Product*) interesting and personalized representations and greater understanding of shared interests or Passions.

2. Completing these as a class contributes to peer collegiality and the climate of the classroom. When students select teachers from other grade levels or subject areas and the brains are displayed in the hallway, it also helps other colleagues to understand how creativity can be a useful part of learning.

3. Younger students may create a brain of their favorite person instead of the teacher brain as they will not have experienced as many teachers.

Extensions: ....

1. See content-based brain activity in Brain Unit section of this book.

2. The entire class might attempt a collage (using pictures from magazines or newspapers) instead of words and drawings to create an interesting visual "class brain" on a wall or bulletin board.

3. Students might also experiment with the notion of a three-dimensional brain in a medium such as paper maché.

4. Students may create brains with multiple intelligence characteristics or right and left brain characteristics (use both right and left templates) as organizers for the brain templates.

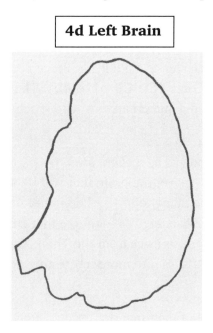

4d Left Brain

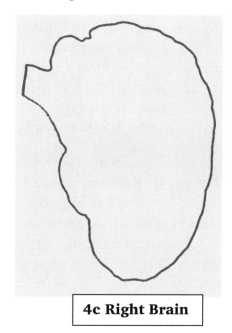

4c Right Brain

4a

Name_____   Date_____

Alpha Think Tank

	/ A	/ B	/ C	/ D	/ E
	/ F	/ G	/ H	/ I	/ J
	/ K	/ L	/ M	/ N	/ O
	/ P	/ Q	/ R	/ S	/ T
	/ U	/ V	/ W	/ Y	/ Z

II Learning and Thinking Style Assessment Activity 1

Activity:	**Multibilities: Class Act I**
Objectives:	1. Students will assess their learning differences and preferences. 2. Students will increase their understanding and tolerance of all learners. 3. Teachers will use this information to plan instruction and to help create an increased awareness and acceptance of these differences.
Strategies:	That's Me, Brain Walk
Elements:	Originality, Elaboration
Fan:	Person
CD:	**Learning & Thinking Style Assessment 1a** That's Me Multibilities CD ONLY **Learning & Thinking Style Assessment 1b** That's Me Multibilities Inventory **Learning & Thinking Style Assessment 1c** That's Me Multibilities Profile Grid

Directions: ....

1. Complete the *"That's Me" Multibilities* **(CD Learning and Thinking 1a)** with the students. Students will stand up and say "That's Me" if the statement you read describes them.

2. *Multibilities Inventory*: Students will self-assess their Multibilities and create an individual grid **(CD Learning and Thinking 1c)** representing their strengths and weaknesses (*Person*). The Multibilities inventory was developed as an extension of the eight multiple intelligence categories by adding the four new areas of the *Curosita Teaching Program*™ to create the *Curiosita Teaching* philosophy of Multibilities. This philosophy includes developing the multiple intelligences in conjunction with four additional categories to be successfully creative: Creativity, Diversity, Practical, and Emotional skills and understandings.

3. Next students complete the Multiple Intelligences assessment scoring grid handout **(CD Learning and Thinking 1c).** Encourage students to fill in their grids with colors and patterns for each category so each will be distinct. Have students display their grids at their desks and then complete a Brain Walk so students can walk around and view each other's Multibilities profiles. With younger students the assessment can be limited to the first eight Multibilities categories. You may also wish to simplify or shorten the statements in each category.

Reflection: ....

Understanding learning differences and interests is especially important in a classroom that is focusing on integrating creativity into teaching and learning. Teachers have the added responsibility of acknowledging the positive and negative characteristics of highly creative students so they can guide them to become more "functionally" creative in the classroom.

Extension:..

1. Divide the class into 12 groups of the Multibilities, and have each group draw a black and white line graphic/logo representing the category to which they are assigned. Work with each group in developing a detailed (*Elaboration*) logo by having mini-conferences to guide them. After you have completed this activity, be sure to save student work examples for the next time you teach this lesson. It would also be useful to create a rubric to assess the logos. Interpreting thinking in visual formats is a process that deepens student understanding of each category the logos represent. Encourage students to use designs from the computer to get ideas they can expand on or reinterpret to help them make meaning of their logos. Remind them that this is not an activity that demonstrates their thinking visually and is not one based on their artistic skill.

2. Wall Graph of Class Multibilities: Duplicate 10 black and white copies of the final logos from each group. Have each group now add color to their logos. Place these on a wall graph to represent the numbers (by tens) on the wall class graph to create a wall-sized Multibilities graph. Have students place their names on each category according to their assessment scores. This now represents the Multibilities of the entire class. It can be referred to in other lesson discussions or used for grouping purposes in any activity. This huge wall graph will be a powerful reminder to the students and all who enter your classroom that we all have different learning strengths and interests.

3. Give students product choices by letting them select those that align with strength areas on their profiles. Use the Multibilities profiles to create teams with opposite strengths for other lessons or activities in the classroom.

4. Using the Multibilitlies Assessment traits formulate journal prompts for each of the 12 areas. You can do this once a week or daily at the beginning of a class year to get to know your students' interests and strengths in each of the categories (*Person*).

1. Verbal Linguistic = VL	7. Intrapersonal = IA
2. Logical Mathematical = LM	8. Naturalist = NA
3. Visual Spatial = VS	9. Emotional = EM
4. Bodily Kinesthetic = BK	10. Practical = PR
5. Musical Rhythmic = MR	11. Differentiation/Diversity = DI
6. Interpersonal = IE	12. Creative = CR

NOTE:

The Multibilites Philosophy was conceptualized as part of the Curiosita Teaching Program™. Its development was influenced by the work of the following individuals:

Dr. Robert Sternberg, Practical Intelligence *Dr. Dan Goleman, Emotional Intelligence*
Dr. Carol Tomlinson, Differentiation *Dr. Howard Gardner, Multiple Intelligences*
Dr. George Betts, Autonomous Learner

That's Me MULTIBILITIES

Rate yourself on a scale from 1 (least like me) to 10 (most like me) for each statement in each category. Each category may total up to 100 pts.

1

___ I read a lot of books!!!
___ I love learning & using new words
___ I can quickly spell words correctly
___ I enjoy Scrabble & word games
___ I talk about ideas with others
___ I like to talk a lot!!!
___ I know one or more tongue twisters
___ I enjoy working crossword puzzles
___ I use big words that sometimes my friends don't know
___ I write stories & poems often

_____ TOTAL VL

2

___ I can do math in my head
___ I do math problems for fun!
___ I say science is the best class
___ I like trying to solve a rubric's cube
___ I can figure out codes easily
___ I play checkers or chess
___ I really enjoy debating my ideas
___ I collect things like stamps, coins, etc.
___ I am really good at using computers
___ I want to know how things work

_____ TOTAL LM

3

___ I like to rearrange my bedroom
___ I can draw a map to another place
___ I daydream to help me think in class
___ I draw & sketch pictures for fun
___ I love movies better than books
___ I ask people to draw a picture when I don't understand an idea
___ I sometimes doodle on homework
___ I can spell words backwards easily
___ I can work puzzles very quickly
___ I can "see" directions to another place in my mind

_____ TOTAL VS

4

___ I exercise almost every day
___ I like learning if we can move around
___ I am good in one or more sports
___ I often tap or wiggle in class
___ I can mimic (copy) other people's walks
___ I have excellent coordination
___ I like to act out stories or plays
___ I talk "with my hands"
___ I am really good at skateboarding or doing tricks on my bike
___ I enjoy building & putting things together

_____ TOTAL BK

That's Me MULTIBILITIES

5

___ I like to hum or whistle while working
___ I have a good singing voice
___ I play several musical instruments
___ I enjoy listening to music with head-
  phones when doing other things
___ In enjoy playing music for people
___ I can sleep listening to music
___ I can tell when people sing off key
___ I notice different rhythms & beats
___ I can remember song melodies
___ I enjoy many kinds of music

_____ TOTAL MR

6

___ I enjoy being around people
___ I can talk easily to people I meet
___ I like working on group projects
___ I am easy for others to understand
___ I am good at solving friends' problems
___ I enjoy group activities and games
___ I understand how my friends feel
___ I am comfortable being in big crowds
___ I like being on a team
___ I have three or more close friends

_____ TOTAL IE

7

___ I am described as strong willed
___ I know what things I can do well
___ I write in a journal or diary
___ I prefer to make my own decisions
___ I know how to take care of myself
___ I enjoy working alone on things
___ I learn when I make mistakes
___ I like to do things my way
___ I seem to sometimes "live in my own
  world" and don't notice others
___ I like to think about or study things
  for a long time

_____ TOTAL IA

8

___ I help my family recycle
___ I like to walk on trails or hike
___ I worry about the environment
___ I enjoy outside or nature activities
___ I like learning about plants & animals
___ I have one or more pets
___ I like being outside better than inside
___ I enjoy camping out in the woods
___ I like working in a garden
___ I can tell when the weather "looks
  like" it is going to change

_____TOTAL NA

That's Me MULTIBILITIES

9

____1. I am happy when others succeed.

____2. I know how my feelings affect my energy level

____3. I can share ideas easily with others

____4. I do not get mad often when working with others

____5. I feel excited when I get to work with others on projects

____6. I can motivate myself to work hard on a project

____7. I stay calm even when it doesn't work the first time

____8. I don't let my feelings stop my thinking

____9. I get energized when working with others

____10. I don't need praise or compliments to keep working hard

_____ TOTAL EM

10

____1. I can see through the "fluff" or not important things to solve the problem

____2. I can quickly find solutions to problems

____3. I get asked by friends often for ideas or solutions

____4. I will try many ways to solve a problem

____5. I can explain how to solve a problem

____6. I can blend friends' ideas to get solutions

____7. I can figure out exactly what the problem is that needs to be solved

____8. I am told I have a lot of practical or common sense when I make choices

____9. I can look at all the options & choices before making decisions

____10. I can solve problems others sometimes can't

_____ TOTAL PR

That's Me MULTIBILITIES

11

____1. I can easily accept different ideas from other people

____2. I value or appreciate opinions of others

____3. I enjoy unusual and different kinds of thinking

____4. I like to work with others who question each other

____5. I like wild, unusual, and weird ideas

____6. I enjoy working with people who have different kinds of talents or skills

____7. I am not bothered when others think differently than I do

____8. I believe slow thinking can be as good as fast thinking

____9. I am open to others' viewpoints & opinions

____10. I can easily change my mind if another person's idea is better than mine

_____ TOTAL DI

12

____1. I have unique and original ideas.

____2. I think of ways to connect unusual things

____3. I like to play with ideas to get better ideas

____4. I ask questions that spark others' interests and thinking

____5. I am very good at brainstorming

____6. I think "can do" when working on problems
and I don't get easily discouraged

____7. I really enjoy coming up with new ideas for
creating things

____8. I get new ideas when I get lost in my daydreams or thoughts

____9. I have a wacky sense of humor and sometimes have to explain my laughter

____10. I have interests in many different things

_____TOTAL CR

Multibilities THAT'S ME: _____

M.I.	10	20	30	40	50	60	70	80	90	100
VL $\frac{1}{}$										
LM $\frac{2}{}$										
VS $\frac{3}{}$										
BK $\frac{4}{}$										
MR $\frac{5}{}$										
IE $\frac{6}{}$										
IA $\frac{7}{}$										
NA $\frac{8}{}$										
EM $\frac{9}{}$										
PR $\frac{10}{}$										
DI $\frac{11}{}$										
CR $\frac{12}{}$										

II Learning and Thinking Style Assessment Activity 2

Activity:	**Multibilities: Class Act II**
Objective:	Students will understand how their Multibilities profile can enhance their learning and career awareness.
Strategies:	Think Tank, Mini-Conference
Elements:	Fluency, Flexibility
Fan:	Product, Person, Persistence
CD:	**Learning & Thinking Style Assessment 2a** Multibilities Think Tank Side A
	Learning & Thinking Style Assessment 2b Multibilities Think Tank Side B
	Learning & Thinking Style Assessment 2c Multibilities Presentation Product and Resource Rubric
	Learning & Thinking Style Assessment 2d Multibilities Test

Directions: ....

1. Students must complete Multibilities Class Act I before starting this activity.

2. Multibilities Part II: Students will create visual photo essay presentations of an eminent person with a Multibilities area of strength that matches a strength area on their profiles. Their essays will depict a time line of how the person became famous.

3. Using the double-sided *Think Tank* **(CD Learning and Thinking 2a, 2b)** students will find "fascinating facts" about the person they selected. Have students label the columns on the Think Tank: Physical, Verbal, Visual, Social, and Mental.

Physical – things you would mostly see them doing

Verbal – things you hear; what they say or discuss

Visual – they way they look or dress; including facial expressions

Social – things or actions they do with others or for others

Mental – things they would think about

Students complete the Think Tanks by searching for 10 facts for each category (*Fluency and Flexibility*).

4. When the Think Tanks are completed the students will meet with a peer and have them evaluate each fact as minus (-) for boring, a plus (+) for interesting and an exclamation (!) for fascinating. They review their scores and search again (*Persistence*) for new facts for those rated with a minus. Then stu-

dents meet with the teacher after making a list of the 3-5 facts they selected as the key facts they want to use for each picture in their presentations.

5. Next students search for 10 photos to support the events or facts they will be presenting about their famous persons (*Person*). Students then will select or research 3-5 or more statements to share with each photo.

6. Final presentations can be put into Power Point, Glogster, or Photostory to share with each other (*Product*).

7. A mini-rubric included in this lesson is used for the final assessment of the product (**CD Learning and Thinking 2c**).

Reflections: ....

The photo essay requirement means that the students can only have photos on their presentation (no words). Students tend to write too many words and read to their audience, and this will make the presentation more interesting. The challenge for the students will be to find powerful photos that "speak to the audience." Teachers should plan mini-conferences with the students to check on their progress during the product development phase.

Extension: ....

This assignment could be used in any content area to depict famous people, places, or events.

Multibilities Test Answer Key:

MATCHING (page 1)		MATCHING (page 2)	
1. F	13. C	1. E	13. H
2. H	14. H	2. G	14. F
3. B	15. G	3. F	15. A
4. A	16. E	4. H	16. B
5. D	17. J	5. C	17. L
6. F	18. I	6. B	18. L
7. B	19. K	7. D	19. K
8. C	20. L	8. A	20. K
9. E	21. J	9. D	21. I
10. G	22. I	10. G	22. I
11. D	23. D	11. E	23. J
12. A	24. L	12. C	24. J

Multibilities Think Tank Side A

2a

Name_____   Grade Level_____

TOPICS:	Physical	Verbal	Visual	Social	Mental
FACT #1					
FACT #2					
FACT #3					
FACT #4					
FACT #5					

NAME_____   GRADE LEVEL_____

TEACHER_____   DATE_____

Directions: Find 10 facts/data about your person that you find very interesting (don't record boring facts). See me for evaluating & scoring the facts you chose for each topic with a peer. Use the front and back of this sheet to record fascinating facts.

Multibilities Think Tank Side B

Name_____   Grade Level_____

TOPICS:	Physical	Verbal	Visual	Social	Mental
FACT #6					
FACT #7					
FACT #8					
FACT #9					
FACT #10					
FACT # PICTURE CHOICES					

The person I have selected for my Multibilities investigation is _____.

The assignment is a presentation of 10 pictures with 3- 5 fascinating facts for each picture for my presentation showing how the person became famous.

_____   _____
Student Signature   Teacher Approval/Signature

_____

2c

Multibilities Presentation Product
Rubric and Resource Rubric

Name_____   Date_____

TASK	1 – 2 pts	3 – 4 pts	5 – 6 pts	7 – 8 pts	9 –10 pts	Product
Presentation of Product	Mumbled Quiet	Rambled Unclear	Needed Prompting	Mostly Clear	Precise & Clear	Points /10
Task Commitment	Minimal Work	Basic Work	Acceptable Work	Extra Effort	Above Beyond	Points /10
Information Facts #	0 - 5	6 - 8	9 - 11	12 - 13	14 - 15	Points /10
Fascinating Facts	Boring	Informa-tive	Interesting	Very Interesting	Fascinating	Points /10
Photos Selection	Not Interesting	Somewhat Interesting	Very Interesting	Visually Appealing	Eye Catching	Points /10
TOTAL POINTS						/50

Person _____

Total Pts. _____   Date Due _____   Date In _____

10% of points will be deducted for late presentations.

2c

Final Facts for Multibility
Presentation Product

Name_____   Date _____

1.

2.

3.

4.

5.

6.

7.

8.

9.

10.

Students: This list should be short versions of your 3-5 facts for each picture. I will use this list to evaluate your product as you complete your presentation. Have this form completed before you present. Good luck. I look forward to viewing your final products!

Multibilities Test

Name_____   Date _____

MATCHING: Match each characteristic to the correct Multibility. There are two answers for each (24 points). Look for the answer that "best fits" each category.

a. visual/spatial   e. verbal/linguistic   i. practical
b. musical/rhythmic   f. interpersonal   j. emotional
c. intrapersonal   g. logical/math   k. diversity
d. bodily/kinesthetic   h. natural   l. creativity

_____ 1. Seems to be "street smart"

_____ 2. Has lots of pets

_____ 3. Hums and whistles to self

_____ 4. Easily reads maps, charts, and diagrams

_____ 5. Moves, twitches, or taps while sitting in a chair

_____ 6. Gets involved in several after-school activities

_____ 7. Likes to have music on when they study

_____ 8. "March to the beat of a different drummer"

_____ 9. Likes to read, write, and talk

_____ 10. Enjoys using computers

_____ 11. Does well in competitive sports

_____ 12. Daydreams often

_____ 13. Enjoys doing projects by themselves

_____ 14. Is concerned about the environment

_____ 15. Plays chess, checkers, and solves Rubik's cubes

_____ 16. Enjoys spinning tales and telling jokes

_____ 17. Doesn't let feelings stop thinking

_____ 18. Can explain how to solve a problem

_____ 19. Is not bothered when friends think differently

_____ 20. Is very good at brainstorming

_____ 21. Works hard without getting compliments

_____ 22. Is good at explaining how to solve problems

_____ 23. Believes that slow thinking can be as good as fast thinking

_____ 24. Has a wacky sense of humor

MATCHING: Match each job or career to the correct Multibility. There are two answers for each intelligence (24 points).

_____ 1. journalist

_____ 2. tax account

_____ 3. salesman

_____ 4. veterinarian

_____ 5. judge

_____ 6. conductor

_____ 7. mechanic

_____ 8. navigator

_____ 9. actor

_____ 10. scientist

_____ 11. playwright

_____ 12. military officer

_____ 13. farmer

_____ 14. counselor

_____ 15. architect

_____ 16. disc jockey

_____ 17. comedian

_____ 18. toy inventor

_____ 19. multicultural teacher

_____ 20. head of jury

_____ 21. investigator

_____ 22. engineer

_____ 23. project manager

_____ 24. team leader

<u>K.M.S.☺. (optional)</u>

CHOOSE ONE OF THE FOLLOWING STATEMENTS: WRITE 5 THOUGHTS. (5 points) USE THE BACK OF THE PAGE FOR YOUR ANSWER TO THE QUESTION.

- The question is no longer "How smart are you?" it's "How are you smart?"

- What is your definition of the last four Multibilities: emotional, practical, diversity, and creative?

II Learning and Thinking Style Assessment Activity 3

Activity:	**Right and Left Brain**
Objective:	1. Students will analyze opposing traits of the Right and Left Brain characteristics. 2. Students will increase their awareness of how their "preferred" traits affect their learning.
Strategies:	That's Me, Anchoring, Brain Walk, Slap-Stick-Review, Mini-conference
Elements:	Fluency, Flexibility, Elaboration, and Originality
Fan:	Person, Product
CD:	**Learning & Thinking Style Assessment 3a** Right and Left Brain Self-Assessment **Learning & Thinking Style Assessment 3b** Right and Left Brain Matching List **Learning & Thinking Style Assessment 3c** Right and Left Brain Graphic CD ONLY **Learning & Thinking Style Assessment 3d** Right and Left Brain Plates - Student Samples (10) CD ONLY **Learning & Thinking Style Assessment 3e** Right and Left Brain Test

Directions: ....

1. Have students take the Right and Left Assessment **(CD Learning and Thinking 3a)** to determine their learning characteristics. When they finish, have students line up on each side of the room according to their highest scores (*Person*). The students in each line should then put themselves in ascending to descending order to further demonstrate the distribution of Right and Left Brain traits within the classroom. Students with Right and Left scores that are the same or nearly the same are encouraged to stand in the middle of the room. Students enjoy this procedure and will express interest in the visual class graph they just completed.

Note: If you are using this to create mixed groups for a specific activity you can assign students standing in the middle to one side or the other to balance the field. An example of this is when you need teams or partners with writing strengths and drawing strengths.

2. Right and Left Characteristics Matching

Give students the list of right and left brain characteristics **(CD Learning and Thinking 3b Right and Left Graphic)**. Ask students to draw lines independently, connecting opposing characteristics. As students finish, tell them to start studying the characteristics (*Anchoring*) with a partner of their choice as they will have a *Right and Left Brain Test* **(CD Learning and Thinking 3c)** in the near future. This study period also prepares students for the review and Brain Walk evaluation of student products that will come later in this activity.

3. Have students team with a partner of opposite strengths and create a mini-poster of right and left brain symbols and words. **(CD Learning and Thinking 3c)**. This could also be done as a Gloster poster on line.

4. Place sets of student Right & Left plate samples on tables. Tell students they are going to do a Brain Walk. Remind them this is a non-talking opportunity. Ask students to rotate from table to table evaluating the Right and Left plates from prior students. Tell them to especially look for plates that demonstrate the element of *Elaboration* and/or *Originality*. Tell them you will cue them when to rotate. Begin the Brain Walk by playing music and assigning groups of students to each table display. Ask students to look for a Right and a Left plate that they believe meets the rating of Knock-My-Socks-Off (K.M.S.☺). Bring students to a group area such as the carpet at the front of the room in a circle formation. Now have students share the plates they selected and share why they choose it.

Note: If this is the first time you are teaching this lesson you won't have prior products. We have included pictures of products as examples **(CD Learning and Thinking 3d)**. The first year you can also have a collection of magazine pictures or clip-art that symbolize some of the characteristics, and have students select and explain how the picture represents a particular characteristic. These also serve as inspirational pictures for the products the students will create.

5. Right and Left Brain Criss-Cross Plates

Next have students select their top three favorite characteristics from each side of the original Right and Left Brain Characteristic list. Have students line up with their lists when they have completed this task. Go through the line of students and have them select their favorite Right brain trait. Next reverse the order of students and ask them to select their favorite Left brain traits. Remind students not to choose a trait that has been selected by another student (duplicate assignments may be given at teacher's discretion). You may have students check off each trait as it is selected so they don't select a duplicate. This also keeps students engaged in the selection process. Set a due date for the project to be turned in – usually a week is sufficient. Tell students final drafts (in pencil) must be approved by you before they add permanent color. The review process is a *mini-conference* with you. Give students points for the draft. This is a critical step in the learning process, allowing teachers to give *formative feedback* (suggestions and questions) and it prevents students from turning in the "five minutes before class project." Initial and date approved drafts. A fun way to display the plates in rooms with drop-in ceiling tiles is with push-pins on the ceiling. Recognize K.M.S.☺. *products* by placing them in the center area or in some particular location for further recognition.

6. Give students the Right and Left Brain characteristic test. **(CD Learning and Thinking 3e)**

Reflection: ....

Knowing more about any type of learning trait empowers students and gives them ownership of their abilities and skills. Recognition of these traits and the constant awareness and acceptance of thinking and learning differently must be ever-present in a creative thinking classroom in order for students to further develop their abilities in these areas.

Note: These activities take place over several days and are not meant to be completed in one lesson.

Extensions: ....

1. Studying the characteristics for the test may be done as a card sort with characteristics printed on cards for table groups to sort. This activity can supplement the somewhat boring yet essential task of learning facts-based memorization items by actively engaging students.

2. Complete a "That's Me" for Right and Left Brains to pre-assess students' understanding or awareness of the Right and Left Brain Learning Characteristics. The questions for this activity can be compiled from re-writing some of the Right and Left Assessment statements and/or the Right and Left Characteristics list in this section (*Person*).

3. Slap-Stick-Review: Divide the class into two teams and have them line up on opposite sides in the back of the room. Put a flip chart on a stand and draw a line down the middle of the paper in the front of the room. Write the word Right on the right side and the word Left on the left side. Put two spatulas on the shelf of the stand. Read a left or right brain characteristic out loud to the class. Next say "Go," and the two students at the front of the line on each team run to the chart, pick up a spatula, and "slap" the word right or left with the spatula to indicate their answer. The student that slaps the correct word first earns a point for their team.

NOTES

> *"The significant problems we face cannot be solved with the same level of thinking we used when we created them."* **Einstein**

3a   Right and Left Brain Self-Assessment

Name_____   Date_____

DIRECTIONS:

Read the following left and right brain characteristics. Circle ONLY the number beside the statements that describe you! Total your answers on the last page.

1. I believe there is a right and wrong way to do most everything.

2. I like to keep a journal or diary of my thoughts and ideas.

3. I find it easy to follow written directions exactly as they are written.

4. I enjoy thinking of many things at once and do not like to focus on one thing at a time.

5. I'm usually wearing a watch and often find myself looking at the clock.

6. I can remember a person's face but often have trouble remembering their name.

7. I like to analyze/study problems and think them through carefully.

8. When comparing things, I usually look for ways they are alike rather than ways they are different.

9. I'd rather take a true/false, multiple-choice or matching test than an essay test.

10. I use my imagination a lot and like to daydream when I am in class.

11. I prefer to read the directions before I try to put something together.

12. I change my mind often and don't like sticking to a schedule.

13. Generally, I like to arrive at class or go to events on time.

14. I like assignments that give me a lot of choices and options.

15. I learn best by seeing and hearing.

16. I learn best by touching or doing.

17. I like to make a list of the "pluses" and "minuses" before making a decision.

18. If I try to remember something, I generally picture it in my mind.

19. I enjoy working with facts and data and don't use hunches to get answers.

---

curiosita teaching Handbook of Instructional Strategies   © *Pieces of Learning*

20.I don't mind taking a chance and will make choices that "feel right" for me.

21. Sometimes I talk to myself when I am learning something for the first time.

22.I often use gestures and express emotions when I am talking.

23.I like to plan my day and enjoy making a list of things I have to do.

24.People have told me often that I'm creative.

25.I like to learn facts, dates, and specifics.

26.I enjoy music.

27.I prefer to know what's going to happen ahead of time.

28.I can easily remember melodies and tunes.

29.I am usually in control of my feelings.

30.I can understand math when using shapes and symbols.

31. I usually can recall information I need quickly and easily.

32.enjoy reading and writing; it comes easily to me.

33.I can really concentrate on one thing and do not get distracted easily.

34.When I work in a group, I can "feel" the moods of others.

35.When solving problems or taking tests, I prefer to go step-by-step to get the answer.

36.It bothers me to stop working on something I enjoy when the bell rings.

37.I can learn new vocabulary words easily.

38.I can spell words backwards by "seeing" them in my mind.

39.I'd probably make a good detective or a lawyer.

40.In class I don't pay attention to what everyone else is doing.

41. I notice and remember details.

42.I can easily see the whole picture when only a few puzzle pieces are in place.

43.I don't mind practicing something over and over until I can learn it.

44.I communicate best with someone "in person" rather than on the phone.

45.I can remember jokes and punch lines easily.

46.I sometimes have trouble concentrating even when I know I should.

47. I can write directions that are clear and easy to understand.

48. I sometimes rely on my feelings when making decisions.

49. I basically have a day-to-day routine I follow most days.

50. I can remember things according to where I "saw" them on the page.

SCORING:

LEFT BRAIN	RIGHT BRAIN
ODD NUMBERS CIRCLED TOTAL =	EVEN NUMBERS CIRCLED TOTAL =

Remember: We are all Right AND Left brained. Most of us just prefer one style of thinking (Right or Left) over the other.

Think of jobs or professions people choose to do. Make a list below of 5 or more for right brain thinkers and 5 or more for left brain thinkers.

LEFT   RIGHT

1. _____   1. _____

_____   _____

_____   _____

_____   _____

_____   _____

3b

Right and Left Brain Matching List

LEFT BRAINS	RIGHT BRAINS
1. Systematic & Serious	1. Prefers Essay Tests
2. Sequential	2. Multitasks
3. Intellectual	3. Emotional
4. Structured & Planned	4. Looks at Whole Problem
5. Controls Feelings	5. Haphazard
6. Analytical & Logical	6. Music & Art
7. Facts & Data	7. Controls Left Side of Body
8. Remembers Names	8. Pictures Things to Think & Learn
9. Time Oriented	9. Look for Similar Things
10. Auditory & Visual	10. Intuitive
11. Controls right side of body	11. Spontaneous
12. Follows Spoken Directions	12. Spatially Oriented
13. Talks to Think & Learn	13. Creative
14. Likes T/T & Multiple Choice Tests	14. Abstract Random
15. Takes Few Risks	15. Kinesthetic
16. Looks for Differences	16. Follows Demonstrated Directions
17. Math & Science	17. Takes More Risks
18. Thinks of One Thing at a Time	18. Remembers Faces
19. Controls Right Side of Body	19. Controls Left Side of Body
20. Breaks Apart Problems	20. Enjoys Humor

3e

Right Brain & Left Brain Test

Name_____   Date_____

Label each term as describing Right Brain **(RB)** or Left Brain **(LB)** functions. There are 5 for each side of the brain. (10 points)

____ 1. Takes more risks   ____ 6. Is creative

____ 2. Looks for differences   ____ 7. Remembers faces

____ 3. Dislikes memorizing   ____ 8. Prefers multiple choice tests

____ 4. Thinks in order   ____ 9. Is spontaneous

____ 5. Controls right side   ____ 10. Thinks concretely

Facts: Label the right and left brain definition below

____ 11. The _____ brain acts as the creative stimulator and controls intuition and pictures.

____ 12. The _____ brain acts like a calculator and controls logic and words.

Circle the five terms that describe <u>Right Brain</u> **(RB)** characteristics.

Analytical	Objective	Arts & Music	Timeless
Cause and Effect	Sequential	Emotional	Visual
	Intuitive	Logical	

OPTIONAL K.M.S.☺.:

Choose one of the quotations below and respond to the following questions:
1. How does it relate to something we have learned in class?
2. How does it relate to being a more "Right" brained thinker or a more "Left" brained thinker?

Circle the quotation of your choice and give me five or more thoughts.

"Not everything that can be counted counts, not everything that counts can be counted."
- Albert Einstein

"All people can learn. Not on the same day. Not in the same way."   - Kallik

"Cogito ergo spud. I think, therefore I yam." - Graffito

OPTION II: K.M.S.☺.

Pick your favorite Right & Left characteristic. Write it on the table below and draw a symbol for each-KMS☺!	
LEFT	RIGHT

II Learning and Thinking Style Assessment Activity 4

Activity:	**Gender Sort**
Objective:	Students will review and discuss the differences in learning characteristics between males and females.
Strategies:	Cards Sort, Quick Write (journal), Tic-Tac-Toe or Choice Board
Elements:	Fluency and Flexibility
Fan:	Product, Process
CD:	**Learning & Thinking Style Assessment 4a** Gender Sort Cards CD ONLY

Directions: ....

1. Have students journal for 3-5 minutes: "How do you think boys and girls learn differently?" (*Person*) What kinds of ways do boys like to learn? What are some choices girls make when they can choose what or how they learn? Have table group discussions, and compile a list of boy traits and girl traits – do not evaluate the correctness of this list at this time.

2. Give student table groups or partners a set of male and female learning traits included **(CD Learning and Thinking 4a)**. One trait is written on each card. The cards are pre-numbered for easy identification for the discussion process. Have students arrange their cards under the male sign and under the female sign (*Process*). Encourage students to disagree/discuss selections. Now read each characteristic, and have a show of hands indicating selections before stating the correct column. If teams or partners do not have the card in the correct column, have them start a discard pile, and remove any incorrect guesses to that pile.

3. Finally, go back to the journal list, and decide if corrections need to be made. Also discuss how the student-generated list has connections to the statements on the cards.

Reflection: ....

Students love this activity! Many of them have casually observed these learning differences since beginning school. Understanding different types of learning characteristics empowers students.

Extensions: ....

Create a Tic-Tac-Toe or Choice Board using the Creative Product lists **(XI Products and Wiki Resources on CD)** and have students complete an assignment (*Product*) from the board on the topic of gender difference. Have students turn in copies of any research they use to supplement the facts in a growing Gender Card Sort Game.

III Brainstorming Activity 1

Activity:	**Brainstorming Dissection I**
Objective:	Students will process a deep understanding of the meaning and purpose of the skill of brainstorming.
Strategies:	Quick Write, Think-Pair-Share
Elements:	Fluency, Originality
Fan:	Process, Persistence, Perception
CD:	**Brainstorming 1a** Brainstorming Student Definition Handout **Brainstorming 1b** Brainstorming Student Definition - Sample CD ONLY

Directions (Part I): ....

1. Ask students to do a 3-5 minute *Quick Write* with the prompt "What is Brainstorming (*Process*)?"

2. Make a common list of phrases or words students generate on flipchart paper and keep it to use later (*Fluency*).

3. Provide students with a copy of the *Brainstorming Student Definition* **(CD Brainstorming 1a)**. (Student Sample **CD Brainstorming 1b).**

4. Ask students to read the complex definition independently and to circle, underline, or highlight words they do not understand.

5. Partner students as a next step (*Think-Pair-Share),* and have them look up the definitions of these words.

6. Provide feedback to each team when reviewing their definitions for accuracy (*context*) before they begin the re-write.

7. Next, ask each team to re-write the entire definition so a much younger student would understand this complex meaning of Brainstorming (*Perception*). Remind them to use the lines below the definition and to make sure they include in their writing a total reinterpretation of each phrase in the original definition.

8. When teams believe they have completed the new definitions and addressed all terms in the original definition, have them meet with the teacher for a *mini-conference* to evaluate their new definitions for completeness and accuracy.

9. The teacher reviews the definition line by line and asks students to state the phrase in their definition that addresses each component.

Directions (Part II): ....

1. When all student pairs have finished Part I, group the class in front of a whiteboard or flipchart, and have a student read the first sentence of the complex definition.

2. Ask partners to read sentences of their re-writes of each section.

3. The teacher and/or groups select the one that fits best for each sentence and write it on the board or flip chart.

4. Now select a final editing team to complete a final draft of the new class definition to post in the classroom. This team may work on this task as the rest of the class returns to work on any Brainstarter as an *anchoring activity*.

Reflection: ....

Brainstorming is the essential overarching process of any creative thinking classroom. It is interesting to note most students have not had much formal or procedural training in using the powerful tool of Brainstorming. Often students have been introduced to the term Brainstorming but do not understand how powerfully it can improve thinking. They do not use the process of Brainstorming correctly with a rigid interpretation of the rules. This often leads to a counterproductive outcome. This is a very intense and complex learning task for students. This complicated definition has been used with middle school-aged students and gifted 3-5 elementary students.

Extension: ....

The definition dissection process may be used for any complex definition that is part of your curriculum. Caution: It is an intense and powerful learning process and should only be used for very important concepts or terms, or it will lose its desired learning effect. This activity also works well to address collaboration procedures and processes such as teamwork, mentoring, coaching, etc.

<u>NOTES</u>

> *"Children become more cautious and less innovative.*
> *Worst of all they tend to change from being participators*
> *to being spectators." Dacey*

1a

Brainstorming Definition Student Handout

1. Students: your challenge is to re-write the following complex definition of brainstorming so that a very young student can understand all the parts of the definition.
2. You are to focus on using words young students can understand and not be concerned with grammar and correct spelling.
3. Your main purpose is to make sure you address each word in your new informal definition.

Brainstorming is a tool for generating options. It involves a deliberate search for a large number

_____

of possibilities to address or deal with tasks or ideas. These are challenges that require new

_____

possibilities and/or different perspectives of one or more individuals. This tool focuses on

_____

producing a variety of options that are unique and novel. Brainstorming is founded on

_____

the principal of deferred judgment in order for all ideas to be elicited freely. It is much

_____

different from everyday conversations, debates, lectures in its purpose and outcome.

_____

Brainstorming is most often used in a group setting but can be successfully used by an

_____

individual. Brainstorming sessions are often guided by a facilitator or experienced group leader

_____

but are also found to be useful for novice individual thinkers. Brainstorming is a powerful tool

_____

that creates synergy and leverage of the combined perspectives of all members of a group. It is

_____

a problem solving and/or idea generation method that uses creative group thinking to generate

bold and innovative ideas.

(Adapted from Center for Creative Learning, Inc. 1998)

III Brainstorming Activity 2

Activity:	**Brainstorming Dissection II**
Objective:	Students will create a personally meaningful phrase and symbol for each of the four rules of Brainstorming.
Strategies:	Brainstorming, Mini-conference, Call-back
Elements:	Fluency, Flexibility, Originality
Fan:	Person, Passion
CD:	**Brainstorming 2a** Brainstorming Rules & Symbols CD ONLY
	Brainstorming 2b Brainstorming Student Phrases - Sample CD ONLY
	Brainstorming 2c Brainstorming Test
	Brainstorming 2d Student Brainstorming Rules and Symbols - Samples (8)
	CD ONLY

Directions (Part I): Discussion ....

1. This activity must follow Brain Storming Dissection I. Pass out the Brainstorming Rules handout **(CD Brainstorming 2a)** and discuss. Student samples: **(CD Brainstorming 2b)**

2. Have a general discussion with the students about the meaning of each of the four rules. Keep this discussion at a generalized level, and address each rule very briefly so students own the concepts and the ideas and are not compromised or led by the thinking of others. The four Brainstorming Rules are:

- Lots of Ideas - generate as many as quickly as you can
- Freewheel - think of "wild and crazy ideas"
- Piggyback - jump onto your own ideas or the ideas of others
- Defer Judgment - do not verbally, visually, physically, or mentally put down the ideas of others

3. Discuss and give examples of negative judgment in each of these four categories:
- Verbal - making negative comment, e.g. "That's dumb."
- Visual - rolling eyes, gestures, faces, etc.
- Physical - walking away, hand slap to head, etc.
- Mentally - having disparaging thoughts

4. Here's a fun way to end this discussion. Have students look at you and say to them, "Now make a sound that shows you don't like something. On three. Ready? 1. . . 2 . . . 3." And then, of course, say, "Now make a sound that shows you really, really like something on three . . . 1... 2... 3."

5. Next say, "Now give the look that shows you really, really like something on three . . . 1... 2... 3." And finally, "Now give the look that shows you really don't like something." Now repeat this process with gestures.

This final effort at recognizing judgment in all forms and intensities is really powerful for students. As a call-back when I overhear students judging others and stopping their thinking, I ask, "What rule of Brainstorming did you just break?" After a while I hear students making the same comment to other students as the course of the class progresses. It is a simple yet powerful process that continues to establish and reinforce the climate of a creative thinking classroom.

6. At this point, talk about the influence of positive judgment on the process of Brainstorming. Ask a student what they think about their idea when the teacher says, "Boy, Caleb's idea was fantastic!" Positive, especially very expressive positive reinforcement or statements during a Brainstorming phase can literally stop the thinking of many of the other students.

Note: During the initial phase of Brainstorming, ideas are generated in a free-flow manner, and any necessary choices or selections are put off until a later time. This is called deferred judgment.

Directions (Part II): Human Graph ....

1. Ask students to line up on the right side of the room if they enjoy and/or are good at drawing. Line-up on the left side if they are good at writing. Line up in the middle if they are good at both (*Passion*).

2. Now have students partner with someone across the room to create a team. Students who line up in the middle can be placed on either side to even up the teams.

Directions (Part III): Creating Symbols (Student samples CD Brainstorming 2d)..............

1. Tell students they are now going to create a symbol and a powerful word or phrase for each of the four rules of brainstorming (*Fluency, Flexibility, Originality*).

2. Have the writers on the teams begin by creating a dictionary chain (reading the meaning of the words and looking up meanings or words in the meaning) of words and/or phrases for each of the four rules. The goal is to create K.M.S.☺. words and phrases for each of the four rules.

3. Let the drawers begin sketching or searching clipart ideas to symbolize each of the four rules. Their final symbols will be hand drawn, but they can use the clipart for idea starters.

4. When finished, teams meet in a *mini-conference* with the teacher for approval of their draft. The teacher initials the draft and gives each team design points before they can add color to their symbols and words/phrases.

5. Tell teams the symbol should be approximately as big as a big paper plate so that it can be seen from across the room. Encourage teams to make words and phrases bold and big.

Directions (Part IV): Wall Collage ....

1. The last phase of this project, after final drafts have been approved for each team, is the class creation of a wall collage representing the four rules of brainstorming on a hallway wall.

2. The final draft of all symbols and words or phrases is done on a light-colored bulletin board paper such as yellow.

3. Trim the individual words and symbols closely, and have students fit them tightly together in a puzzle format with the four sections grouped representing the four rules.

Directions (Part V): Brainstorming Test (CD Brainstorming 2c) ....

Administer the Brainstorming test to students.

Reflection: ....

This personal interpretation of Brainstorming creates an emotional connection between the learning and the students. Remind students that this is not purely an artistic activity. Students are encouraged to search for idea symbols or clipart on the web that they can re-create and embellish upon with their own drawings. The wall collage creates an impressive visual interpretation of the importance and under-standing of the Rules of Brainstorming. It is a powerful reinforcement for the climate of the classroom.

Extension: ....

In any subject matter a visual interpretation and personally meaningful phrase will connect the students to a deeper understanding of the event, concept, etc. This type of activity is particularly appropriate and effective in the content areas of science and social studies.

NOTES

"Not only does there appear to be no loss when providing creative learning, there may actually be some very important gains."
Isaksen

2c

Brainstorming Test

Name_____   Grade Level_____

List each of the four Brainstorming rules and give a brief definition (in your own words) (8 points).

1. _____ definition:

2. _____ definition:

3. _____ definition:

4. _____ definition:

Why are the rules of Brainstorming an important part of our thinking classroom? (3 Points).

Give a visual and verbal example of someone breaking the 4th rule of Brainstorming (4 points).

OPTIONAL K.M.S.☺.:
What makes a person creative? Give 5 or more thoughts on the back of this page. How do creative people contribute to our world?

III Brainstorming Activity 3

Activity:	**Creative Brainstorming**
Objective:	1. Students will generate a number of ideas within a given category.
	2. Students will practice the "rules" and process of Brainstorming.
Strategies:	Press, Brain Dump, Brainstorming, Think-Pair-Share
Elements:	Fluency, Flexibility, Originality
Fan:	Perception, Press, Persistence
CD:	none

Directions: ....

Prior to conducting this activity, it is necessary to teach students the four major "rules" of Brainstorming. Since the major purpose of Brainstorming is to generate lots of ideas, this process is a simple and effective method to use on a regular basis as part of the instructional content of the lesson or as a "stand alone" process. When used as a stand-alone process, this tool is an excellent method for infusing the classroom with the daily dose of Flexibility and Fluency to improve the malleability of the brain and increase the efficiency and speed of thought. This tool also serves to develop the *Perception* of students as they make new extended connections to each topic. Here are the rules.

- Many Ideas. The more ideas you have, the better the chances of having some good ones. Strive to get past the easy or obvious ones.
- Freewheel. Do not hold back ideas even if they seem wild, crazy, or strange. Sometimes these can be modified and made workable.
- Piggyback. Make creative connections or spin-offs of ideas already put forward by other members of the group. Think of them as extensions or Elaborations.
- Defer Judgment. Keep an open mind. Judging ideas will get in the way of generating them! Remind students to watch their body language and their expressions.

1. Divide students into groups of four.

2. Have students select a scribe or recorder (someone to record the group's answers).

3. Now have students list all the birds they can in 2 minutes (*Press*).

4. At the end of two minutes, have the scribe draw a line under the last answer recorded.

5. Now allow the group another minute (*Press*) to generate additional answers.

6. After students have generated further answers during the additional minute, share with them the concept that during the first two minutes they were practicing the "Brain Dump." In other words, they were tossing out all the easy and common answers they could think of quickly. Students will find that the answers generated in the last minute are often much more original than the ones generated in the

first two-minute session. Students will recognize the role played by Press, as they are being timed and repeatedly challenged to strive for more ideas (*Persistence*).

7. Score one point for each *common* answer and three points for each *original* answer. The teacher can be the judge, or students can all take a turn in this role to further understand and practice the recognition of highly creative answers.

8. Examples of birds that are *common* answers: any bird (robin, wren, blackbird, raven, crow, ostrich, chicken, etc.).

Possible *original* answers include creative, unique, or novel (*Original*) birds or ways to use the concept "bird." Examples include: a jailbird, the Thunderbirds, Woody Woodpecker, Tweety Bird, Big Bird, Admiral Byrd, the Partridge in a Pear Tree, etc.

Reflection: ....

The tool of "Brainstorming" has been around since the 1940s, when advertising executive Alex Osborn developed it as a formal process for his employees to use to generate new ideas. It remains a universal and basic tool in creative thinking, designed primarily to teach people the need to generate numerous alternatives as we go about the problem solving process.

This tool is part of the foundation of a creative thinking class. Using it often will increase students' expertise in thinking. It is an enjoyable tool that develops thinking and adds a layer of competition to energize the outcome. As students become involved in the choice of topics, it may be useful to keep a Brainstorming Box in the front of the class so topics can be drawn for quick and easy brainstorming sessions.

Brainstorming is a tool that has been loosely applied in many teaching situations. Students may have been told to "go brainstorm." Without a deep understanding of the meaning, purpose, and process (see Brainstorming Dissection I and II), it is a somewhat ineffective tool. It is a skill that can be honed and further developed with additional tools (SCAMPER, Think Tanks, Pass Arounds, etc.). With practice, it becomes a "power tool" for improving student thinking!

Extensions: ....

1. As above, divide into groups of four. Have students select a scribe. Continue to encourage students to generate original answers. However, if they become "stuck," generate common answers to keep the process moving along.

- List all houses you can in 2 minutes.
- List all the fish you can in 2 minutes.
- List all the trees you can in 2 minutes.
- Have students brainstorm categories to brainstorm!

2. The topic for the creative brainstorming can be "creatively" attached to content areas of study. Here are examples:

- Things that are green (rain forest unit)
- Things that are related to space flight
- Things that can be found in the sea
- Words an engineer would use

3. Have students draw, write down, or generate orally *all the things they can think of that are* red.

Possible answers include:

- Stop sign
- Crayon
- Pool ball
- Pencil
- London bus
- Tomatoes
- Strawberries
- Nail polish
- Lip stick

4. Again, the object here is to generate a number of answers (Fluency). Other activities (do one a day) are to *list all the things they can think of that are*:

- Round
- Yellow
- Flat
- Green
- Make noise
- Round foods
- Begin with the letter "m"
- Begin with the letter blend "cl"

- Words that end with the suffix "ism"
- Words beginning with "c" but sound like "k"
- Name as many "feeling" words
- Begin with the letter "b"
- That use electricity
- Words that mean "heavy"
- Kinds of sandwiches

5. Curricular and Content Extensions: Depending on the area of study, this activity can be used to pre-assess or introduce a new area of study. It can also be used formatively and as a post-assessment exercise across all content areas. Examples include:

- States that begin with the letter ____
- Countries or cities in Europe

- Mammals
- Things that live and grow in the Amazon

6. Another adaptation is an ABC version with students naming something from the next letter of the alphabet. For instance, the task could be to *name anything from the book they just finished reading* as a language arts assignment. Students in teams of two take turns stating anything related to the story they just read. If a team cannot come up with something for that letter after 90 seconds (Press), a chance is given to the next team. Points are awarded for correct answers.

This recall activity could also be used for any unit of study in any content area as a fun game summary or review. These can be completed individually, with a partner, or in small groups (Think-Pair-Share). They can be generated orally or in written form.

NOTES

> *"No amount of training will create a da Vinci or Edison. But it is also true that everyone's capacity for creative living and creative thinking can be increased." Davis*

III Brainstorming Activity 4

Activity:	**Pass Around**
Objective:	Students will generating various answers using the characteristics of an object to stimulate their thinking process.
Strategies:	Brain Dumping, Brainstorming, SCAMPER
Elements:	Fluency, Flexibility, Originality
Fan:	Press
CD:	none

Directions: ....

1. Divide into groups of six or eight students.

2. Begin by selecting a *flexible object* like a pipe cleaner, belt, scarf, necktie, or a newspaper.

3. Begin to pass around the object. Each person must give an idea for what the object could "creatively" become.

For example, begin with a pipe cleaner. The first student holds the object and says, "This is not a *pipe cleaner*, it is a _____." Creative answers might be:

- a diving board for an ant's swimming pool
- a giant's toothpick
- a spoon to stir the soup
- a teacher's pointer
- a stick of firewood
- a propeller for a very small helicopter.

4. Then the first student passes the pipe cleaner to the next student, and they repeat the process. Students may skip a turn *one time only* if they can't think of an answer. They should provide an answer next time.

5. Pass the object around the group four or five times (*Fluency*) so the students can generate multiple ideas.

6. To conclude the activity, have each group share what they considered to be the best idea generated (*Originality*).

Directions: Run Around..

1. This is a team game version of the Pass Around activity. It adds the dimensions of physical movement and a light-hearted competition to the thinking exercise.

2. Line up the students in two groups on each side of the room. The lines will merge at the back of the room to form the starting line for the activity.

3. Put two of the objects selected on two chairs placed in the center at the front of the room.

4. When you say "Go," the first two team members run to the chairs and grab the objects.

5. Once holding the object, they proceed to say, "This is not a _____, it is a _____."

6. The teacher acts as the referee and award points for creative or K.M.S.☺. answers.

Reflection: ....

During this activity it is a good time to remind the students of the brain technique of Brain Dumping. This activity works well throughout the year. With practice it continues to hone the creative thinking skills of students. It can also be used within the context of many curricular areas of study.

Extension:..

1. Do a "Fortunately" & "Unfortunately" story. Have each student get a partner. The first person says, "Fortunately, a large box was delivered to my front door this morning." The next person says, "Unfortunately, it was raining and the box got terribly wet." The first person continues, "Fortunately . . ." and so on.

2. Pass around an *inflexible object*. A pencil, ruler, or cup works well. Answers are often more creative as students cannot bend the object but are restricted to its current form and shape.

3. Use sensory inputs (*Press*) to get the "creative juices of the students flowing." Here are a few prompts:

- You are in a rainforest.
- The object is hot.
- The object makes a noise.
- It is something from a favorite book or movie.
- It is a part of an animal.
- It is something that is used outside.
- It is from the medieval times.

4. Adding some of the SCAMPER letters is very useful when trying to get students to generate additional answers. Using letter prompts from SCAMPER for different rounds of this activity stimulates student thinking, e.g. you might ask students to MAGINFY their answers. For the inflexible object this may generate ideas like Empire State building, etc.

IV Elements of Creativity Activity 1

Activity:	**Elements of Creativity**
Objectives:	1. Students will generate a number of creative responses (divergent thinking) through the imaginative use of shape and form. 2. Students will identify and understand the four Elements of Creativity and their relationship to the Rules of Brainstorming.
Strategies:	Think-Pair-Share, Brainstorming, Call-back
Elements:	Fluency, Flexibility, Originality, Elaboration
Fan:	Press, Person, Perception
CD:	**Elements of Creativity 1a** Blank Elements of Creativity Handout **Elements of Creativity 1b** Flexibility Sample **Elements of Creativity 1c** Originality Sample **Elements of Creativity 1d** Combined Sample **Elements of Creativity 1e** Elaboration Sample **Elements of Creativity 1f** Elements of Creativity Definitions CD ONLY **Elements of Creativity 1g** Creative Circle Student Teaching Samples (4) CD ONLY **Elements of Creativity 1h** Creative Shapes for Elements Handout CD ONLY

Directions (Part I): ....

1. Tell students: "As of right now I will answer no questions." Tell them that for this activity they are to do their own work (no talking, no looking at someone else's paper, etc.). Distribute the *Elements of Creativity* Activity handout **(CD Elements 1a)** face down. Inform students that when you say "Begin" they are to turn over their papers and make objects out of the circles. You may (depending on the age of students) want to draw an example of a "clock" (things drawn inside the circle) or "flower" (things drawn outside the circle) on the smart board, overhead projector, or flip chart paper. When you say "Begin" allow students 10 minutes (*Press*) to create circle objects.

2. After 10 minutes, ask them to look carefully at the objects they drew, and select the one they believe no one else in the room has on his or her paper. Ask them to put an "X" or an asterisk " * " next to it. Now allow them to share their circles with a partner or at their table with classmates. Tell the students to look at the objects they created and to discuss the four Elements of Creativity.

3. *Fluency* is the number of responses generated. Randomly ask students how many objects they created. When they respond, say to them, "That's exactly the number you should have." Repeat this statement to each student as they respond. In this exercise, if a student used 17 circles, then their Fluency score is 17. If they completed 11 circles during the 10-minute time limit, then their Fluency score is 11. An important point to make with students is that whatever their Fluency score is, it is exactly what it should have been. Should they try a similar exercise again, they should attempt to improve on their pre-

sent Fluency score. This is an "individual competition" or practice towards improving their skill in the area of Fluency.

4. *Flexibility* is the ability to generate items or answers that fall into different categories. Display the page of the circles that are all foods **(CD Elements 1b)**. Ask students to discuss with a partner what they see. They should soon realize these items are all foods. Next ask students to exchange their papers with a partner to try to group or categorize their responses into similar groups (examples: foods, things with wheels, balls, faces, etc.) by labeling their drawings. Do a quick share going around the room, and ask each student to call out a category.

5. *Originality* is the "uniqueness" or "one-of-a-kind" nature of the item. Next ask, "Now, who will be my risk taker? Who will share the one they marked as one they believe no one else in the room has created?" Risk taking is one of the characteristics of the creative person (*Person*). Call on four or five students to share and see how unique the responses are. Younger students are often very eager to share. Older students may initially be somewhat hesitant. After each student shares, ask "How many students drew this example?"

Discuss the relative originality of each item, e.g. 1 in 25, 7 in 25, etc. After each student shares their most original drawing and records their originality "ratio" you may want to create a human graph, lining students up from ascending to descending originality ratio. When doing this part of the activity you may have to first recognize (stand up) the students who had 0 out of 25, and then complete the human graph with their next best ratio, as you will often find many students will have at least one item that has only been drawn by them on their paper.

Discuss with students the role relevance plays in Originality. Ask what conditions would change the level of Originality? The discussion may result in students realizing the outcomes will be affected by 1) assigning a different task, 2) changing the group members, or 3) altering group size. Should you have 25 students in the class each generating 20 items during the 10 minutes, and one child creates something no one else in the room has created, his/her unique or novel item may well be 1 in 500!

Now display the sample that shows objects created using one or more than one circle **(CD Elements 1c)**. Ask students, "What do you notice about this sample?" Then ask, "Who made objects using more than one circle?" Call on students to share. Should any student create an object by combining two or more circles, they receive "bonus points" for Originality! (e.g. a snowman, a traffic light, a bicycle, a pair of glasses, etc.).

This is why you stated in the beginning of the exercise, "From now on you may ask me no questions!" If you had allowed questions, you can bet the first question would have been, "May we combine the circles?" and then everyone would do so. What we are looking for here are the risk takers–those students willing to combine circles when that was not specifically addressed in the directions. Ask students to think for a minute as to why they did not attempt to combine circles. This is a good time to bring up the concept of risk taking and how it is respected in your classroom and how it affects a person's creativity. These could also be good journal prompts for the next day of class. This may also be a good time to interject that in the creative classroom there is often no one right answer or point of view.

6. *Elaboration* is the amount of detail supplied by the student for each item. You might discuss at this time that Elaboration is a skill that actually impedes initial Brainstorming. Begin a *Think-Pair-Share* by asking the students, "How might Elaboration affect Brainstorming?" Display the sample that shows three

drawings with incredible detail **(CD Elements 1e).** Tell the students that the person who drew these objects was given the same directions as they were and the same amount of time. Now have them discuss with a partner and then with the whole class to complete the Think-Pair-Share.

Students will notice and describe the details of each drawing, such as:

1. some of the individual states are drawn on the globe
2. the details of the clown's face and clothes
3. each bicycle wheel has 16 spokes

In this activity, Elaboration is recognized by adding more details to the drawings. Someone may draw a simple flower, while another student might draw a more complex flower with many petals, flower parts, etc. There are many factors related to the Elaboration. Students who like to draw or who pay attention to details might naturally demonstrate more Elaboration. It should also be noted that on a timed activity, there could be less Elaboration than on one involving more time. It should also be noted that a student who uses more Elaboration during a timed activity would usually complete fewer circles, resulting in a lower Fluency score.

Have students individually select their most elaborate object drawn. Then have them select the most elaborate object at their tables. Now, as a group, select one object that is not very elaborate, and take two minutes to expand on it by adding more details. Discuss the idea that elaborations (for the purposes of this activity) are not right or wrong – they are just another way of thinking! Now talk about how Elaboration, when demonstrated appropriately, can Knock-The-Socks-Off (K.M.S.☺.) a teacher. Details in story writing and product creation add interest and excitement to products. These questions are also good as journal prompts for the next class period.

7. Tell students you did this activity once with a group and, after about one minute, one person turned his paper over and said he was finished. Display the sample with a squiggly line drawn around all 25 circles. **(CD Elements 1d)**. Tell the students this is what the person drew. Ask the students, "What do you think it is? At your table, make a list of things this picture could be." Students will generate a list of ideas such as: cookies on a cookie sheet, egg cartons, a Band-Aid, the Connect Four game, a bath mat, etc. Now ask them to guess the answer given by that student. The answer was: "The last thing a fly sees (a fly swatter)!" The class will erupt in laughter.

8. Discuss the diversity of thought and different perspectives (*Perception*). Ask students how they think this student came up with this kind of idea. Ask if they believe this student thinks differently from others. You might further ask, "Did this student do it right or wrong?" You can further discuss how humor, creativity, and risk taking are essentials for success as an entrepreneurial creative thinker.

Directions (Part II): ....

1. Start with the following Think/Pair/Share journal prompt: Compare and contrast the Rules of Brainstorming with the Elements of Creativity. The goal is five or more thoughts. Write for two minutes (*Press*).

2. Next find a partner (a "brain;" another student you haven't worked with before) and try to generate 10 or more thoughts. Work together for two minutes.

3. Now create a class list of the comparisons between the Rules of Brainstorming & the Elements of Creativity (Call-back).

4. Post student answers on a whiteboard or flipchart.

5. Call-back: Ask students: "What rule of Brainstorming is like Fluency?"   (*Answer*: Many Ideas)
   Call-back: Ask students, "What Brainstorming rule is like Flexibility?"   (*Answer*: Free Wheel)
   Call back: Ask students, "What rule of Brainstorming is like Elaboration?"   (*Answer*: Piggyback)
   Call back: Ask students, "What rule of Brainstorming relates to Originality?" (*Answer*: Free Wheel)

Reflection: ....

This lesson is a foundational lesson for students to begin to understand how the Elements of Creativity are the underlying constructs of creativity. This lesson cannot be rushed! Teachers are encouraged to bring parts of this lesson into future lessons as Call-backs or reminders of these essential ingredients of creativity.

When this lesson has been presented to adult educators, they responded as to how powerfully it assisted them in understanding how creativity can be taught using the Elements in any content area. This lesson will take approximately one hour to complete. Teachers are especially encouraged to "script teach" this lesson when introducing it for the first time to any group of students.

Note: Four samples of student work are available on the CD **(CD Elements1g)**. This lesson has been adapted from E. Paul Torrance's work in creativity assessment. We have developed this activity into an instructional lesson that teaches students the Elements of Creativity.

Extensions: ....

Repeat the activity. Push students to create more answers after "dumping" their first answers (*Press*). Now that they know they may combine circles, there may be even more creative products.

1. "Create a Picture." Another drawing activity is to have students create a picture: (students are practicing *Fluency, Originality,* and *Elaboration*).

using only exclamation points   using only numbers   using only letters
using only straight lines   using only a single color   using world signs
using information from content/subject areas

2. Call out categories and have students make round (circles) objects in that category. Examples include: foods, toys, gardening, music, sports, math, etc. (students are practicing all four *Elements of Creativity*).

3. Use a sticky dot. Tell students to place the dot anywhere on a blank sheet of white paper. Tell them to draw a picture including the dot. The dot can become a nose, a wheel, the center of a flower, the sun, etc. Students are practicing *Originality* and *Elaboration*.

4. Use this set of directions to repeat the activity at different times using the Creative Shapes handouts: sets of circles, squares, triangles, or parallel lines provided (students are practicing all four *Elements of Creativity* **(CD Elements 1h).**

Elements of Creativity Handout

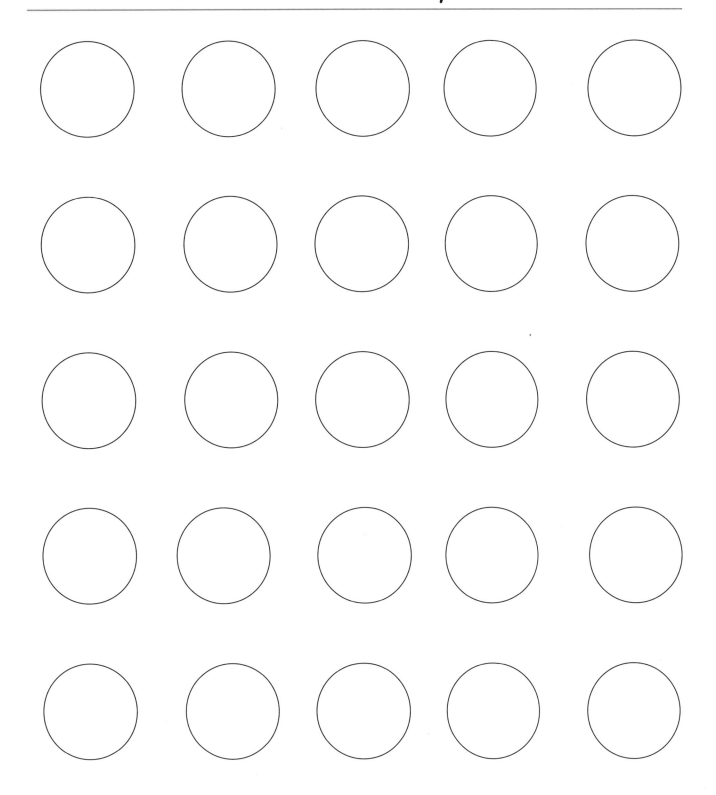

Flexibility

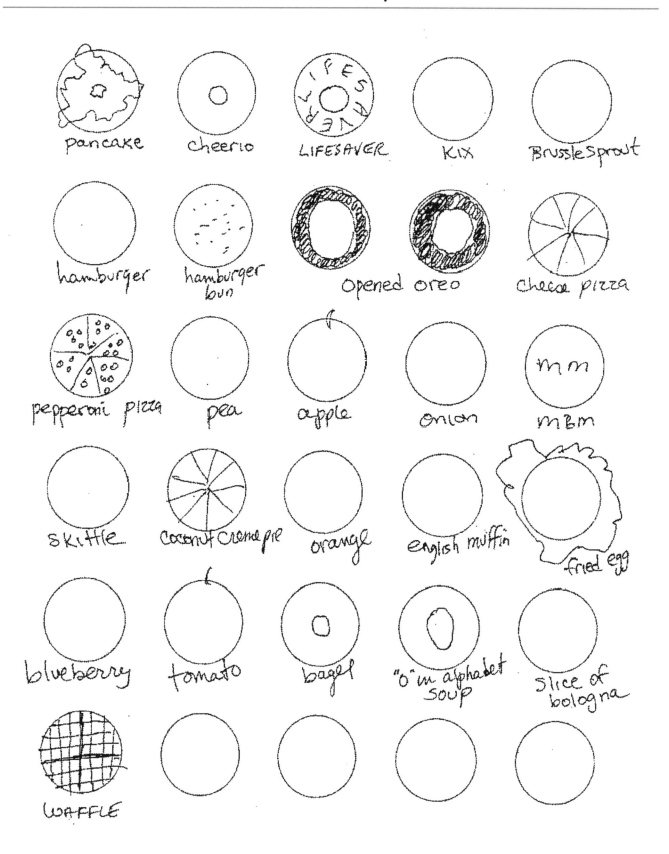

© *Pieces of Learning*

Originality

1c

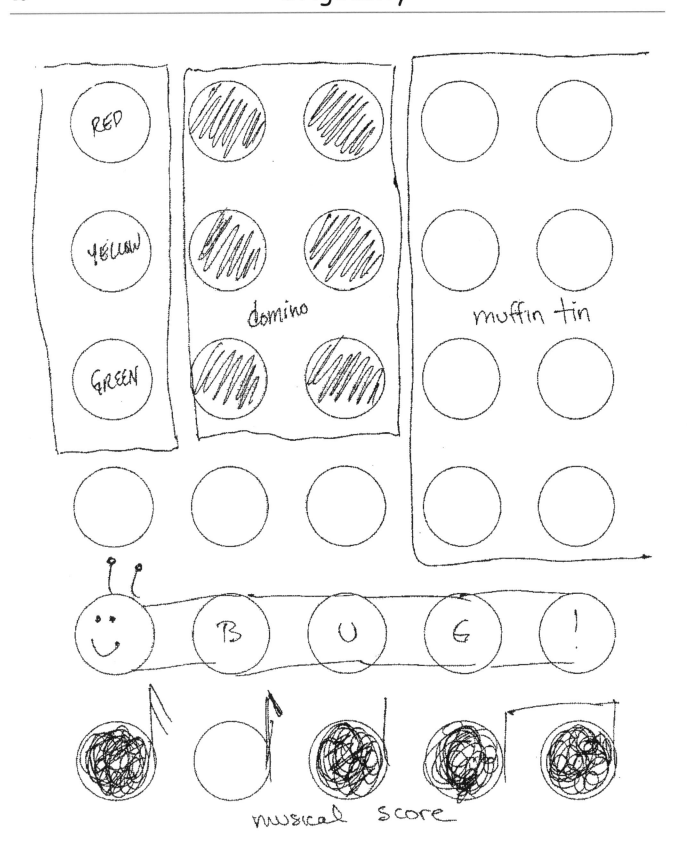

1d

Combined

Elaboration

1e

V Elements of Creativity Activity 2

Activity:	**Creativity Myths**
Objective:	1. Students will create visual representations of each of the four myths of creativity. 2. Teachers will refer to the myths during parts of instruction to dispel their relationship with creativity.
Strategies:	Brainstorming
Elements:	Originality, Elaboration
Fan:	Person
CD:	**Elements of Creativity 2a** Creativity Myths Handout

Directions: ....

1. Give each student a *Creativity Myths (Person)* handout **(CD Elements 2a)**. They will work with a partner of their choice or one chosen by the teacher to complete the activity. On one side of the sheet in each box the students write words or phrases to explain the meanings of each myth (*Brainstorming*). On the other side is a corresponding box in which they will draw a collection of visual images (*Originality*) that also represent each myth.

2. Once the sheet is completed, give the students a set of 4" x 6" index cards (one for each myth). They will pencil draft their symbols or visual representations on scrap paper and tape them to the un-lined side of the cards. They will then write the creativity myths they represent and their definitions of that term on scrap papers and tape them to the lined side of the index cards. The students are encouraged to create detailed images (*Elaboration*) and powerful definitions of each term (*advanced vocabulary*). Once the teacher approves the drafts, students write their final words or phrases on one side of the cards and create their symbols with full color on the other side of the cards. It is helpful for each team to be composed of someone who likes to draw and someone who prefers to write and/or compose.

3. Myth Game: A class set of cards is placed on the table with the drawing side face up. One set of partners selects two cards they believe to represent the same myth. If they guess correctly they get to keep the cards. If not they must replace them. All partners get turns at selecting. The team with the most cards at the end is the winner.

Reflections: ....

This activity helps students understand the meanings behind the myths associated with creativity. After teaching this class several times, the teacher will have multiple sets of cards that will make the game more challenging and interesting for the students. Remind students when they are in the process of creating a visual image that this is not a drawing class and that they are free to trace or copy free clip art for their drawing symbolizations of each myth.

Extensions: ....

Put sets of the myths cards on the shelves or area you set aside as a problem solving station so students can have frequent practice at making the correct choices.

Creativity Myths

Mystery – Creativity is a rare form of genius possessed by only a few people. It comes from some outside source and you cannot control it. We know so little about it. It's puzzling.

Magical/Mystical – Creativity is an elusive phenomenon that evaporates or vanishes if you try to look at it too closely or study it in depth. We believe it to be ethereal. Creativity involves trickery, not substance.

Madness – Creative behavior is bizarre, bordering on mental illness. Creative individuals are strange, odd, and weird. We view it as an anti-social or unhealthy behavior.

Merriment – Creativity involves behavior that is totally spontaneous and undisciplined. It doesn't happen with any forethought or planning. We use it only to entertain and surprise us.

Myths Handout

Myths: Words or Phrases	Myth Symbols
Mystery	Mystery
Magical/Mystical	Magical/Mystical
Madness	Madness
Merriment	Merriment

V Creative and Critical Thinking Activity 1

Activity:	**Creative and Critical Thinking**
Objective:	Students will dissect the definition of creative and critical thinking to better understand the processes.
Strategies:	That's Me, Brainstorming, RE-D☺, Mini-Conference
Elements:	Fluency, Originality
Fan:	Perception, Product
CD:	**Creative and Critical Thinking 1a** That's Me CD ONLY
	Creative and Critical Thinking 1b Thinking Definitions
	Creative and Critical Thinking 1c Student Samples CD ONLY
	Creative and Critical Thinking 1d Acrostic Poems
	Creative and Critical Thinking 1e Acrostic Poem - Student Samples CD ONLY
	Creative and Critical Thinking 1f Creative and Critical Thinking Test

Directions Part I: That's Me...

1. Complete the *Creative and Critical "That's Me"* **(CD Creative and Critical 1a)** with students to pre-assess their understanding of the Creative and Critical Thinking processes.

2. Read each statement and say, "Stand up if you think this is true" for each item (*Perception*)

3. Give students the correct answer, but do not allow questions or provide additional explanation at this time. At the end of this process, tell students the questions were deliberately written to be somewhat ambiguous to get them to really think about the "thinking meanings" of each process.

Directions Part II: Definitions & Game

1. Pass out the complex definition of *Creative and Critical Thinking* **(CD Creative and Critical Thinking 1b).**

2. Ask students to highlight, underline, or circle the important words or phrases in this definition.

3. Next, have students re-write the definitions of *Creative Thinking and Critical Thinking* in their own words to create simple definitions of the terms. **(CD Creative and Critical Thinking 1c)**

4. Now have students generate 10 examples (*Fluency, Brainstorming*) each of creative and critical thinking opportunities to demonstrate they know how to apply these thinking processes. Each list must have five from the school setting and five from the home setting.

5. Next, have all students gather near the center of the classroom to play the Creative and Critical Game. Read a random statement from the school and home creative and critical thinking opportunities

from a student's list. You may also want to have your own list of situations to infuse in this activity or a collection of your favorites from your student products portfolio.

6. As you read each statement, students are to move to the right side of the room if they think it is a *Creative Thinking Opportunity* or to the left side of the room if they think it is a *Critical Thinking Opportunity*.

Directions (Part III): Acrostic Poem ....

1. Give students the assignment of creating an acrostic poem (*Product*) for each of the words Creative and Critical (see example **CD Creative and Critical Thinking 1d**).

2. Now tell students you want them to use the Dictionary Chain process. This involves looking up terms and then looking up words in the definition to create a "chain" or list of new, interesting, and powerful words or phrases for each letter. Encourage them to be creative in the word choices (*Originality* – see *Elaboration* on the **CD Creative and Critical Thinking 1e** - sample poem). The words they select should reflect the meaning of creative and critical for each poem.

3. Show students a few student work products and/or **CD Creative and Critical Thinking 1e**. The poems will be graded on visual appeal, impact of words and phrases, and correct use of terminology (meanings). Below is a short rubric to use for this assignment.

CREATIVE & CRITICAL ACROSTIC POEM RUBRIC TOTAL POINTS = _____						
POINTS	**0**	**1 - 2**	**3 - 4**	**5 – 6**	**7 - 8**	**PTS.**
VISUAL APPEAL	NONE	SOME EYE CATCHING	MOST EYE CATCHING	ALL EYE CATCHING	K.M.S.☺	
WORD IMPACT	NONE	SOME POWERFUL	MOST POWERFUL	ALL POWERFUL	K.M.S.☺	
MEANING MATCH	NONE	SOME	MOST	ALL	K.M.S.☺	

Directions Part IV: Creative and Critical Thinking Test (CD 1f) ....

1. Remind students they will have a test on Creative and Critical Thinking (in this section) so they will remember to study or review these terms.

2. Administer the test.

Reflection: ....

This "dissection" of creative and critical definitions is similar to the process used for introducing Brainstorming. These are short definitions, but when students search the dictionary for compatible words or synonyms of words in the definitions, it is a very effective process. It deeply embeds an understanding of the original terms. Students look up the word in the first definition, and continue to look up words in each definition found, until they discover the one that best explains the terms from their perspectives.

The Creative and Critical game energizes students with movement, and when the students separate to each side of the classroom, the immediate class graph helps demonstrates their understanding of the concepts. These are examples of supporting learning with brain-based applications of movement and visual representations of thinking.

NOTE: It is imperative you really take the time to examine each student response. Many times you will be surprised by their answers. Sometimes you will think their answers do not make sense or you cannot see the connections. When this happens, schedule a mini-conference to ask the student to explain their thinking and their answers. By doing so, you will either see that that have indeed missed the point and you can ask them to RE-D☺ the assignment, or, more likely, you will experience the wonderful phenomenon of students sharing amazing creative connections.

Extension: ....

Use this process with any complex definition or term from any content area.

NOTES

> *"The one thing the experts do agree on is that creative skills can be developed, techniques can be taught, and an individual's creativity can be enhanced with practice." Biech*

Thinking Definitions

Creative Thinking

It is a mental and social process involving the generation of new ideas, connections, or meanings between existing concepts. It is an assumption-breaking process that occurs through encountering gaps, paradoxes, opportunities, challenges, or concerns and then searching for meaningful new connections by **generating**:

Divergent thinking for:

- Many possibilities

- Varied possibilities

- Possibilities from different perspectives

- Unusual or original possibilities

- Details to expand or enrich possibilities

Critical Thinking:

It is a mental process of discernment, analysis, and evaluation. It involves reflecting upon an idea, decision, or task with solid, common sense judgment, examining possibilities carefully, fairly, and constructively, and then **focusing** you thoughts and actions by:

Using convergent thinking for:

- Organizing and analyzing

- Synthesizing and reconstructing

- Refining and developing promising possibilities

- Reviewing with relevance and logic

- Ranking or prioritizing options

- Choosing or deciding on certain options

(Adapted from the Center for Creative Learning, Inc. 1998)

Acrostic Poems

Cool ... Crazy

Radical thinking

Exploring emotions

Allow for dreaming

Time don't matter

Infinity of thoughts

Visionary ventures

Elaboration exponential!

Conclusion driven

.....

Reality focused

Inside the box

Terminating thoughts

Iron it out

Catch the problem

Analyze it

Let's be logical!

$$\left(\sum_{k=2}^{n-1} \frac{n!}{k!(n-k)!}\right)+1$$
$$n,k \geq 2$$

Creative & Critical Thinking Test

1f

Name_____ Grade Level_____

Directions: Give an example of when you have used or could use creative thinking and critical thinking at home and at school. Give DETAILS!

THINKING	SCHOOL	HOME
CREATIVE		
CRITICAL		

Directions: Label the following words as: A. Creative Thinking or B. Critical Thinking (5 answers each).

_____ ORGANIZING   _____ MANY

_____ ANALYZING   _____ REFINING

_____ PRIORITIZING   _____ ORIGINAL

_____ UNUSUAL   _____ VARIED

_____ DETAILS   _____ DECIDING

OPTIONAL K.M.S.☺.

ON THE BACK: List and define the four Elements of Creativity. Give five thoughts about how using the Elements of Creativity improves our world.

V Creative and Critical Thinking Activity 2

Activity:	SCAMPER & REPMACS
Note:	Dr. Don Treffinger has given permission to use the telephone activity SCAMPER in this book. The processes, procedures, and all other activities are original.
Objective:	Students will learn to improve their brainstorming by using a check-list tool.
Strategies:	Mini-Conference, RE-D☺, Brainstorming, Brain Dump, PMQ, Think-Pair-Share, Anchoring
Elements:	Fluency, Flexibility, Originality, Elaboration
Fan:	Persistence, Press, Product
CD:	**Creative and Critical Thinking 2a** SCAMPER Tool Handout **Creative and Critical Thinking 2b** Predictions of the Future Past CD ONLY **Creative and Critical Thinking 2c** REPMACS Handout **Creative and Critical Thinking2d** SCAMPER Best School in the World - Student Sample CD ONLY **Creative and Critical Thinking 2e** Word & Name Checklist CD ONLY **Creative and Critical Thinking 2f** REPMACS Test

Directions: ....

Have students complete Brainstorming Dissection I and II activities before introducing SCAMPER.

Directions (Part I): REPMACS ....

1. We are going to introduce the SCAMPER checklist Brainstorming tool by teaching it to students using a <u>reverse</u> process. Give students a blank *SCAMPER Tool Handout* **(CD Creative and Critical Thinking 2a).** Go through each letter of the SCAMPER handout and explain what type of change each letter stands for Note: one of my very creative 8th grade students named this process REPMACS (SCAMPER spelled backwards).

2. Start by displaying the following quotation on the white board or flip chart paper **(CD Creative and Critical Thinking 2b)**:

"This telephone has too many shortcomings to be seriously considered as a means of communication. The device is inherently of no value to us."

3. Show students a set of photos of telephones from all ages and stages of development over the last 100 years. Ask students to focus on the Element of *Elaboration* and brainstorm a list changes (*Think*) in the phone that these photos bring to mind for the next 90 seconds (*Press*). Note: they won't be able to see visually all the technical changes, but the photos should jog their thinking. Hand out the *REPMACS Handout* **(CD Creative and Critical Thinking 2c)** and have students write the following question in the prompt box: *What changes have been made to the telephone?* Now let them work with a partner (*Pair*)

to decide which change fits best with which letter of REPMACS. Remind students they cannot use the same example for more than one letter.

4. Bring the class together and do a class REMACS (*Share*), eliciting suggestions from all students for each letter. If a student proposes a change that does not fit well for the letter selected, prompt them to find a better fit for the suggested change. You can have more than one example for the letters as you post them on the combined SCAMPER.

5. Tell them that they have processed a *reverse SCAMPER* and that from now on we will refer to this thinking process as REPMACS.

Directions (Part II): School SCAMPER ....

1. Assign students to SCAMPER their school as homework. The goal is to use this checklist process to *make your school the best; the greatest school in the world*. Students can use the blank *SCAMPER Tool Handout* for this task **(CD Creative and Critical Thinking 2d).**

2. Have a mini-conference with individual students to assess their use of the SCAMPER letters for this task. At this time it would be good for the rest of the class to be working on an Anchoring Activity. If a student has incorrectly given an example for a letter, ask them to explain how they made this choice for this letter. Sometimes their explanation is very logical and does support the correct thinking process. This is a very powerful moment in teaching and learning as it demonstrates teacher flexibility and also dissects a student's thinking – which sometimes is inaccurately assessed.

3. If a student has not given a correct example for a letter, this is a good time for the RE-D☺ process. This allows the student more time to practice and use each letter correctly. They are also understanding and practicing the learning power of revision and continuous effort (*Persistence*).

4. Next have students cut apart the suggestions for each letter of SCAMPER from their homework sheet. Sort all the answers into each letter to form seven groups (one for each letter): S, C, A, M, P, E, & R. Divide your class into seven groups and assign each group one letter. Have each group prioritize the suggested changes from the one they like *most* to the one they like *least*. Groups may also discard any they believe are duplicates or not appropriate for the letter.

5. Create a new class SCAMPER of changes that can be made to the school (*Product*) using the top idea from each category. If one or more of the changes addresses the same concept, select the second or third idea to use on the combined class SCAMPER.

6. Finally introduce the idea evaluation tool of PMQ and have groups of students process each suggested top change. The questions generated could be used for future journal prompts, table discussions, or debates. It might be interesting to forward these ideas to the administration or staff for further thought. The PMQ activity directions are included in this section of the Handbook (V Activity 3).

Directions (Part III): Brainstorming SCAMPER...

1. Line up students equally on both sides of the room with the lines meeting in the middle of the back of the room. Place two chairs at the front of the room with neck ties hanging from them.

2. Tell the students they are going to participate in a physically active Brainstorming activity. They must run to the front of the room, pick up the tie, and physically demonstrate their answer to the challenge question.

3. First challenge question: "What could a tie be substituted for?" When the teacher says "Go," each pair of students runs up to the tie and says, "This is not a tie. It is a _____." (E.g. a *jump rope*, and then they *pretend to jump rope*).

4. When the entire class has had a turn say, "Here we go again!" The first ideas were called a Brain Dump (see Introduction section page 19 of this text) as students gave the easy answers. Now the students are going to be challenged to stretch their thinking by repeating the same task with a prompt.

Ask students to repeat the activity and to focus on the 2nd and 3rd rules of Brainstorming: *Freewheel* and *Originality*. Repeat the above activity and acknowledge unique or unusual answers.

5. Now have students use SCAMPER letters. Begin with the letter "M" from the SCAMPER checklist. "M" can represent magnify or minify. Tell students in this round they are to think of minify, and give them the example, "This is not a tie; it is the eyelash of an ant."

6. Have students incubate their thinking for 60-90 seconds (*Press*) and do another round. Repeat this round and tell students "M" now stands for magnify. So, "This is not a tie; it is a support of the Golden Gate Bridge." Again, give students 60 – 90 seconds to incubate their thinking. Continue this activity using the letters "S" and "C" of the SCAMPER check list.

7. All the letters of SCAMPER do not work well for this particular activity. The letters we listed work best. The letter "S" has already been covered in the first two attempts. Now repeat another round for the letter "C." Tell students they must combine something with the tie to come up with a new use, e.g. "This is not a tie; I am combining it with a bamboo pole and it is a fishing rod."

Directions (Part IV): SCAMPER Test ....

1. Give a SCAMPER test over the next week or so to check for understanding.

2. The sample test included is a REPMACS on the telephone **(CD Creative and Critical Thinking 2f).** I have used this as the test and have been amazed at how many students miss some items on this test as it was thoroughly completed in the classroom as the beginning activity! Answers are open-ended, and teachers use judgment as to what answers belong in each category.

REPMACS Answer Key (There are many answers - teachers must judge.)

Reverse Rearrange - now have caller ID seeing who is calling you

Eliminate - the cord

Put to other uses - email

Magnify/Minify - can call world-wide and minify the phone is smaller

Adapt - the dialing numbers are touch instead of rolling

Combine - with a camera or music player

Substitute - texting for writing

3. Other items can be used for a SCAMPER test or a REPMACS test.

Reflections: ....

SCAMPER is a powerful thinking tool and has great flexibility in its use. This type of thinking process very precisely fine-tunes a student's thinking - especially their analytical processes. This is a great example of how using a tool can focus and improve the outcome of any Brainstorming activity.

The student sample school SCAMPER **(CD Creative and Critical Thinking 2d)** was completed in 2006. Interestingly, enough you will notice some of their suggested changes are becoming real today.

Extensions: ....

SCAMPER can be used in a variety of content areas:

- Language Arts SCAMPER: a creative writing assignment
- Social Studies SCAMPER: around changes in societies
- Home Economics: changes in clothing styles or recipes
- Science SCAMPER: inventions
- Students can also create their own SCAMPER checklist using their names or other **(CD Creative and Critical Thinking 2e).**

NOTE: *The original SCAMPER process was developed by Alex Osborn and Bob Eberle. Permission to use the telephone SCAMPER telephone activity was granted by Dr. Don Treffinger. When using, it should be credited as follows: Treffinger, D. J. & Nassab, C. A. (2005). Thinking Tool Guides (Rev. Ed.). Sarasota, FL: Center for Creative Learning. You may use the example, provided that it is credited accordingly.*

<u>**NOTES**</u>

> *"Millions say the apple fell, but Newton was the first to ask why."*
> ***Bernard Baruch***

Initial Task or Question

S	SUBSTITUTE Use for or do instead of?
EXPLAIN	

P	PUT TO OTHER USES Use another way/purpose?
EXPLAIN	

C	COMBINE Join or put together?
EXPLAIN	

E	ELIMINATE Take away or do without?
EXPLAIN	

A	ADAPT Change or do differently
EXPLAIN	

R	REVERSE/REARRANGE Do differently or backwards. Change order or function?
EXPLAIN	

M	MAGNIFY – MINIFY Make larger or smaller?
EXPLAIN	

REPMACS

2c

Initial Task or Question

M	MAGNIFY – MINIFY
	Make larger or smaller?
EXPLAIN	

R	REVERSE/REARRANGE Do differently or backwards. Change order or function?
EXPLAIN	

E	ELIMINATE Take away or do without?
EXPLAIN	

A	ADAPT
	Change or do differently?
EXPLAIN	

C	COMBINE
	Join or put together?
EXPLAIN	

P	PUT TO OTHER USES Use another way/purpose?
EXPLAIN	

S	SUBSTITUTE
	Use for or do instead of?
EXPLAIN	

2f

REPMACS Test

DIRECTIONS: Choose the **best example** for each letter. You **cannot use an answer twice**. Write the word for each letter and then explain your change and how it relates to that letter of REPMACS!

R

EXPLAIN

How has the telephone changed?

E

EXPLAIN

A

EXPLAIN

P

EXPLAIN

C

EXPLAIN

M

EXPLAIN

S

EXPLAIN

V Creative and Critical Thinking Activity 3

Activity:	***PMQ: The Pluses, Minuses, and Questions (+ - ?) Tool***
Objective:	1. Students will learn to evaluate the positives and negatives of a decision or opinion. 2. Students will practice posing questions regarding a decision or opinion.
Strategies:	Brainstorming
Elements:	Fluency, Originality
Fan:	Press, Process, Perception
CD:	**Creative and Critical Thinking 3a** PMQ Log **Creative and Critical Thinking 3b** PMQ Sample Problems CD ONLY **Creative and Critical Thinking 3c** PMQ - Student Samples CD ONLY

Directions: ....

1. Create small groups of three to five students each. Have each group of students select someone in the group to be a recorder and someone to be a timekeeper.

2. Put forth an idea for the groups to explore. For example: *Should schools allow students to have cell phones without restrictions?*

3. Handout the *PMQ Log* sheets **(CD Creative and Critical Thinking 3a)** for students to use to record their thoughts. For two minutes (*Press*), the group is to generate as many pluses (positives, good points, advantages, pros) as it can about the idea. The purpose here is to generate lots of ideas (*Fluency*) by using the thinking tool PMQ to guide students in processing their ideas. Remind them during this brainstorming process, there is *deferred judgment*.

4. Continue the PMQ process by having the teams generate the minuses (negatives, bad points, disadvantages, cons) of the idea for another two minutes.

5. Put up two flip chart sheets and have teams post their positive and negatives on each sheet. Remind them as they post to discard any duplicate ideas.

6. Now for the third two minutes, the group should list as many related (interesting) questions as they can generate surrounding the idea. The following sentence stems are helpful in this part of the process:

"How could . . .?"   "How would . . .?"   "What would happen if . . .?"

"How might . . .?"   "Wouldn't it be funny if . . . ?"

7. Have the table groups discuss the questions. Next have students form partners. Have each set of partners take one of the generated questions and evaluate it in light of more pluses and minuses. Add these new ideas to the Plus and Minus Flip Charts.

8. The final collaborative step is for students to rank each of the charts from the perspective of the most valued or most interesting from each participant's point of view. Give each student three (or more depending on the volume of ideas generated) colored dots to "spend" (vote for) in each chart. Then a set of partners can be assigned to each chart to tally and rank the ideas from the ones receiving the highest votes to the lowest votes. After this stage is completed there is a new opportunity to discuss the results.

Reflection: ....

It should be noted here that the primary intent of this tool is not to change students' minds; rather, it is designed to unemotionally and without bias *explore* ideas of ALL participants. The exploration may result in a change of position (*Perception*) about an idea or a degree of change in viewpoint or perspective related to an idea. This tool can be used in many classroom applications. It is a very powerful tool for teaching students the power of collaboration and teamwork skills.

Extension:..

The PMQ is also useful for exploring any topic, group decision, or situation that has happened, is happening, or will happen. The process helps students keep their minds open to new understandings and new possibilities!

What is really interesting about this process is that a Pluses, Minuses, and Question (PMQ) tool can be completed about every single idea generated by the initial process! Talk about exploring an idea! New ideas and thoughts usually spark questions, and the design of this tool allows for those to be listed along with group evaluations of the idea. These questions can serve to generate further discussions on the topic or thought or guide students in their decision making process.

(SAMPLE)

3a

PMQ Log

PLUSES (+)	MINUSES (−)	QUESTIONS (?)

V Creative and Critical Thinking Activities 4

Activity:	**Choice Boards**
Objective:	Students will learn how to make decisions using a procedural and criteria-based instrument.
Strategies:	Decision Making, Attribute Listing
Elements:	Fluency
Fan:	Process, Product
CD:	**Creative and Critical Thinking 4a** Choice Board Blank **Creative and Critical Thinking 4b** House Choice Board CD ONLY **Creative and Critical Thinking 4c** Pets Choice Board CD ONLY

Directions: ....

1. Students must first think about and select a decision they need to make and would like to work on. Examples include: where to go on a family vacation, what family pet to get, or where to live. These might also be situations where students are asked for their input or opinion. For the students themselves, a decision may be which sport to play, which musical instrument to play, what to major in at college, what part-time job to take, what career to pursue, who to vote for in the upcoming student council election, or even what book to read for a school assignment.

2. Once the topic choice has been made, students are ready to complete a blank *Choice Board* **(CD Creative and Critical Thinking 4a)**. The Choice Board has columns across the top where students can list a number of possible choices. For example, when deciding on a pet **(CD Creative and Critical Thinking 4c)**, the choices might include a hamster, a horse, a dog, a cat, and fish as possible appropriate pets. Down the side of the Choice Board, students will list attributes/characteristics they really want (pluses) in this choice. They then list things they do not want (minuses) in the choice.

3. Each choice is then rated (scored) on a 1-5 scale.

4. A unique feature of the Choice Board is the fact that you also award extra points to the things that are most important in both the positive and the negative categories. These extra points are awarded in the K.M.S.☺. section. Simply "double" the scores of the most important things.

5. Finally you arrive at a total score. The highest score is the choice you should *logically* make based on information and data. Remember, this tool is designed to provide you with information without emotion. You can make better decisions when emotion is temporarily set aside using this tool to *process* decisions or choices.

Reflection: ....

Students are asked many times to make or to help make decisions. When this occurs, they (and we) often, and very naturally, make our decisions hastily and emotionally. This Choice Board is a tool that can help put emotions aside for a brief period of time while looking at the situation with logic and information. Additionally, once students have been engaged in a period of creative activity and have generated many ideas (*Fluency*), the next step is to make a choice and/or evaluate a *Product*. This tool helps students develop evaluation skills.

Extension: ....

Choice Boards may be used to make a variety of decisions and or to evaluate Products.

NOTES

> *"Don't tell your pupils too much. Give them a chance to find out something for themselves. Let the mind have a chance to develop by doing such work. The mind that never has an opportunity to work will not grow." The Normal Instructor, 1895*

Choice Board

OPTIONS

		SCORING OF CHOICE BOARD					
	PLUSES +						
	MINUSES −						
	+ KMSO						
	− KMSO						
TOTAL SCORE							

Score each choice with a 1-5 for how you believe it meets each of your criteria in the Pluses and Minuses. Reminder: each minus attribute must start with the word **NO** and cannot be the opposite of any of the pluses.

VI Think Tanks Activity 1

Activity:	**Think Tanks**
Objectives:	Students will learn to use a graphic organizer to stimulate the production and/or the organization of thoughts and facts.
Strategies:	Brainstorming, Brain Write
Elements:	Fluency, Flexibility, Originality, Elaboration
Fan:	Press, Product
CD:	**Think Tanks 1a** Think Tank Blank
	Think Tanks 1b Foreign Language CD ONLY
	Think Tanks 1c Science Rocks CD ONLY
	Think Tanks 1d Social Studies CD ONLY
	Think Tanks 1e Health CD ONLY
	Think Tanks 1f Math CD ONLY
	Think Tanks 1g Creative Story Think Tank CD only
	Creative Writing Story Starters Blank
	Think Tanks 1h Creative Writing - Student Sample CD ONLY
	Think Tanks 1i Sensory CD ONLY
	Think Tanks 1j Alpha CD ONLY

Think Tank Versions

A variety of Think Tanks are provided for several diverse instructional and planning tasks. The following Think Tanks have been created for different purposes. An explanation and directions for use of each follows, along with templates for each Think Tank.

1. Creativity Think Tank

2. Content Think Tank

3. Creative Writing Think Tank

4. Sensory Think Tank

5. No Problem Think Tank

6. Innovation Think Tank

7. Alpha Think Tank

Creativity Think Tanks

Directions: ....

1. Assign students to groups of three-five team members. You should have four or five teams of students.

2. Use the blank *Think Tank* handout **(CD Think Tanks 1a)** provided when introducing this activity to students. Give one Think Tank handout to each team and ask the teams to select a recorder. There is space for *five categories* going across the top and *five letters* down the side.

3. When using this activity for the first time, select the categories and letters to use for the Creativity Think Tank. Teach the Creativity Think Tank by beginning with very general categories – ones with which every student should be familiar. For example: *fruit, vegetables, colors, candy,* or *beverages.* (You probably don't want to begin with categories such as *South American generals of the 18th century!*)

4. Once the student recorder for each team has written down each category (all teams play with the same categories), announce the letters for this game. For example: A, C, E, R, & S. Wait for the team recorder to fill in these letters on the grid. These letters are totally random, and you may select any (all teams will play with the same letters) you want.

5. Announce to the teams, "You will now have five minutes to complete the Think Tank by filling in each square with a word that begins with the letter to the left under each category heading (*Press*). For example: a *fruit* that begins with *A* is *apple*. A *candy* that begins with *R* is *Reese's® Pieces.* Choose only ONE ANSWER per square!

6. Time the students. Say "Stop" when five minutes have elapsed.

Scoring:

Once the time limit (five minutes in this example) is up, teams will give their answer for each square in the grid.

- If no answer is provided, then zero points are scored.
- If two or more teams have the same answer, then five points are scored.
- If a team has an answer that no other team has (*Originality*), then 10 points are scored.
- The maximum score in a game is 250 points (25 ten-point answers).

When engaged with the Creativity Think Tank Game, students are practicing the following Elements of Creativity: *Fluency* by completing as many squares as they can, *Flexibility* because those squares involve different categories, and *Originality* because they try to come up with unique answers to get the additional points.

This Creativity Think Tank is very similar to the No Problem Think Tank in the Climate Activities section of the Handbook Activity 3. They have similar scoring systems, but the No Problem game has very structured categories and does not involve the random letters down the left side of the Think Tank.

Variations:

   1. When the category is *candy* and the letter is *R,* you may choose to accept *Baby Ruth®* as an acceptable answer.

   2. You can vary the time limit (10 minutes, 30 minutes, a day, a weekend, etc.). The time limit depends on your purpose for doing a Think Tank!

   3. You can control the categories and the letters, or the letters may be chosen randomly (draw from a hat, have each team call out a letter, etc.).

   4. You can push the bounds of your students' creative thinking by allowing teams to put two or three words in each square. This way they may produce more creative, descriptive (*Elaboration*), or unique answers. If you add this component, you can call it a Knock-My-Socks-Off (K.M.S.☺.) answer and award the team 15 points when you think the answer is above and beyond creative. Remember, you are the referee and make all decisions regarding the answer's "worthiness," especially when awarding additional K.M.S.☺. points. Students love this and have a lot of fun trying to make a K.M.S.☺. hit answer for you!

Content Think Tank

Directions: ....

   1. Have students complete the Content Think Tank according to your purpose or goal for the learning activity.

   2. The Content Think Tank has a variety of instructional uses. It can be organized and creatively adapted for the purposes of:

   - research, as a data collection tool when students are beginning to explore a subject or topic,
   - a review tool, as students re-examine material covered in a lesson, unit, or term. Students can work on this for a longer period of time, say two-three days. Students may also work individually, with a partner, or in a small group, and
   - pre or post assessments. For this type of Content Think Tank, the categories at the top of the grid are usually pre-assigned by the teacher. You may allow students to gather facts from a text and/or the Internet and create their own categories around a particular subject of study.

   3. The following sample templates for Content Think Tanks are included:

   - *Foreign Language* (words) - categories: Part of Speech, Synonym, Number of Syllables, Phonetic Spelling, and Tense. **(CD Think Tanks 1b)**
   - *Science* (study of gems) **(CD Think Tanks 1c)** - categories: Color, Hardness, Birthstone Month, Location, and Value.
   - *Social Studies* **(CD Think Tanks 1d)** - categories: Rivers, Cities, Exports, Countries, and Leaders.
   - *Health* (food facts) **(CD Think Tanks 1e)** - categories: Calories, Carbohydrates, Sodium, Fiber, and Fat.
   - *Math* (algebraic equations) **(CD Think Tanks 1f)** - categories: $2x+3$, $3x+4$, $2x+5$, $4x+2$, $x+3$. The "letters" down the side are 1, 2, 3, 4, & 5. Students insert the number into the equation and write their answers in the appropriate squares. For example, the first square would be $2x+3$, where $x=1$, so the answer is 5.

Creative Writing Think Tank

Directions: ....

1. Distribute a copy of a blank *Creative Writing Think Tank* **(CD Think Tanks 1g)** to each student. Put these categories at the top: character, object, plot, setting, and moods. Students may Brainstorm or Brain Write (see Handbook Introduction page 20) words to complete the Creative Writing Think Tank.

2. After completing the Creative Writing Think Tank, students roll dice to come up with new and interesting story combinations as "story starters" for creative writing assignments. Have students do 10 trial combinations and write a summary sentence for each creative story. If a student rolls a six they can choose from any of the choices in the column.

3. A completed *Creative Writing Think Tank* student sample is included **(CD Think Tanks 1h)**. It shows three combinations of dice rolling:

> 1-4-3-2-2: Silly person, box, gets lost, tree house, on cloud nine

> 5-5-3-4-4: Lady bug, marble, gets lost, grave yard, giggle

> 3-5-4-1-3: Starfish, marble, going on vacation, park, awesome

4. Students are very excited to use this stimulating process for getting ideas for writing creative stories. You can also tie the choices to content areas like science and social studies.

Sensory Think Tank

Directions: ....

1. Label the columns of the *Sensory Think Tank* with the five senses: Touch, Taste, Smell, Hear, and See **(CD Think Tanks 1i)**. Complete the Sensory Think Tank in partners or small groups using recall at the end of a unit or as an investigation/research of text material or extension/enrichment outside of the text. The Sensory Think Tank can also be used for creating descriptive writing assignments. To use for this purpose students would visualize a picture of their story in their heads. As they hold this image in their minds they complete each column of the Sensory Think Tank. For example, ask students, "What do you see in your picture that you can smell?" After all columns are completed the students then use these sensory inputs to make their writing more descriptive and interesting.

No Problem Think Tank

Directions: ....

This *No Problem Think Tank* is designed to be used to creatively deal with classroom management situations. If you are basing your teaching on creative thinking, it seems logical to do the same for classroom rules and procedures. The No Problem Think Tank directions and sample have been included in the Climate Activities section of the Handbook (#3 No Problem Activity).

Innovation Think Tank

This version of the Think Tank is a somewhat intense process for most students. It is recommended that you attempt this after students are very comfortable with using the various forms of the Think Tanks.

Directions: ....

The full instructions are included in the next activity of this section of the Handbook as a separate activity.

Alpha Think Tanks

Directions: ....

1. Distribute a blank *Alpha Think Tank* to each student **(CD Think Tanks 1j)**.

2. Have students complete and share according to the purpose of the activity.

The Alpha Think Tank can be used both for re-call or research, as well as for creative idea or thought generation. It is designed using the original Think Tank grid without any row or column headings. The handout incorporates a pre-alphabetized grid. An Alpha Think Tank with 25 letters of the alphabet (minus an "X" in the sample) is provided. You may give the students choices in which letter they wish to omit.

A simple use of the Alpha Think Tank is to have students think of characteristics and/or facts about a person or individual. For example, if they are studying a famous person, they may use the Alpha Think Tank to collect facts about the person beginning with that letter. Once completed, they have a "data base" as they proceed to create the *Product* of a biography or a life time line. Another creative use of the Alpha Think Tank is to have the students use it for listing interesting facts about themselves.

Reflection: ....

Think Tanks are one of the most flexible tools that can be used in a creative learning classroom. Experiment with using the Think Tanks in different ways and for your instructional purposes.

Extensions: ....

The Think Tanks described in this section have numerous uses. The processes described for use by students are ones you may modify and expand to fit your curriculum. As you do so, your students (and you) will experience powerful, fun, and challenging thinking processes!

NOTES

1a

Think Tank

Name _____   Date _____

	/	/	/	/	/
	/	/	/	/	/
	/	/	/	/	/
	/	/	/	/	/
	/	/	/	/	/

curiosita teaching Handbook of Instructional Strategies

Creative Writing Story Starters

Name _____ Date _____

Students will roll the dice to come up with interesting combinations for a creative writing assignment. Have students do ten trial combinations and write a summary sentence for each creative story idea. Then students meet with the teacher for discussion and approval before beginning to draft their creative story.

1. _____

2. _____

3. _____

4. _____

5. _____

6. _____

7. _____

8. _____

9. _____

10. _____

Teacher mini-conference/
approval on _____ (date)   _____
                                        Teacher signature

VI Think Tanks Activity 2

Activity:	**Think Tanks: Innovation Creation**
Objective:	1. Students will use random objects as idea generators for new innovations. 2. Students will participate in all levels of Bloom's Taxonomy of thinking.
Strategies:	Brain Walk, Think-Pair-Share, Force Fit, Brain Share, Brain Writing
Elements:	Elaboration
Fan:	Press
CD:	**Think Tanks 2a** Living & Non-Living **Think Tanks 2b** Innovation Creation **Think Tanks 2c** Living & Non-Living - Student Sample CD ONLY **Think Tanks 2d** New Ideas Innovation Creation - Student Sample CD ONLY

NOTE: This activity takes three or more class periods to complete.

Class Period One

Directions (Part I): ....

1. Show students two photos of living and non -living things on a whiteboard or overhead.

2. Do a *Think/Pair/Share*. Ask students to individually generate five or more characteristics (attributes) of each. Tell them to focus on the Element of Elaboration so they can begin to list characteristics (attributes) of each item for 90 seconds (*Press*). Then pair with a partner for 90 more seconds, and generate 10 or more characteristics of each item.

3. Tell students to circle, underline, or highlight the most interesting characteristic they listed for each of the items.

4. Do a Quick Share and generate a list of characteristics underneath each photo. Tell students they might think of this as reverse *Elaboration*, as they will be striving to describe minute details that already exist to help them generate a list of characteristics (attributes) of each object.

5. Number the final list sequentially as below.

Example: Skateboard + Elephant =

<u>Skateboard</u>

1. rolling
2. wooden
3. friction sounds
4. tips up
5. portable

<u>Elephant</u>

12. gigantic
13. large ears
14. bendy long trunk
15. bugles
16. wrinkled

---

6. colorful	17. smelly
7. energizing	18. slow
8. inflexible	19. tiny tail
9. rectangle shape	20. bony tusks
10. transports	21. good hearing
11. entertaining	22. uses fuel/food

New Ideas/Innovations:

1. Tell student to combine two-three characteristics to create a new idea or a way to improve/change an object or idea to create something new and useful (Force Fit).

2. Provide one or more examples to share. For example:

- 10 + 12+ 1 = an inner city people mover that holds couples
- 13 + 5+ 21 = portable large ear cups that allow nature lovers to hear sound from miles around in the woods
- 10 +15 = a skateboard that sounds a bugling noise to warn people on sidewalks

3. Now have students pair up and pick one living and one non-living object and complete the activity above at their tables.

4. Have the class do a Brain Walk to walk around and view the new ideas created by other partners. Share in a circle group at the end of the class. Ask students to share the most interesting characteristic and/or new idea they observed during the Brain Walk. Close with a discussion of the need and reason for innovation in our world.

Class Period Two

Directions (Part II): ....

Read the following to the students:

Dr. Edward de Bono is a very famous and rich creative individual. Companies hire him to work with teams in their businesses to improve on or make new products. A major car company once asked him to work with a team of engineers to design a new suspension system (the system that makes cars run smoothly on rough roads). Dr. de Bono first asked the engineers to make a model car with square wheels. He next asked them to design the best suspension system they could for this car that had square wheels. Ask the students why they think he had the engineers work with a square-wheeled car.

Answer: After some trial and error and discussion students will arrive at the idea that if engineers could make a suspension system that made a square-wheeled car run smoothly, and then put the same system on a round-wheeled car, it would work even better! This might also a good time to discuss the phrase *"creativity is always simple and logical in hindsight!"* The result of this experiment was that the company now had the best suspension system in the world for cars at that time.

1. Put students into table groups of three to five students each.

2. Give each student a double-sided blank Think Tank: *Living and Non-Living* (**CD Think Tanks 2a**).

---

3. Choose categories of *living* and *non-living* things for each of the five columns. When choosing the categories keep in mind you want them to include somewhat elaborate items so students can generate many characteristics/attributes. Examples include: Mammals, Flying Things, Growing Things, Vacation Places, Hot Things, Sports Objects, Technical Devices, Articles of Clothing, Pets, etc.

4. Have students label both sides of the paper with the same column headings.

5. Now tell students to generate ideas in each box below the columns (follow Brain Writing rules). Remind them to use both sides of the paper.

6. Call time when most columns are filled.

7. Instruct students to cut out each box and place them in a tub at the front of the room.

Class Period Three

Directions (Part III): ....

1. Distribute a blank double-sided Think Tank *New Ideas Innovation Creation* to each student. **(CD Think Tanks 2b)**

2. Label the columns **T-H-I-N-K** and number the rows **1-5**.

3. Tell students they are going to play the Innovation Game using the ideas they generated from the last class.

4. Draw two slips from the idea tub, and begin filling the Innovation Creation Think Tank with living and non-living things on one side of the Think Tank. You can choose to use or discard ideas from the drawn slips to give students the most interesting combinations.

5. Discard duplicates and fill the board systematically: Row 1, 2, 3, 4 and 5. Make sure all students place the same two items in exactly the same box as they are creating a class game board.

6. Now play the Innovation Game. Begin by putting "New Ideas" in the opposing box on the back of the game board. Remind students to focus on the characteristics (attributes) of the items or objects to assist them as they are creating new innovations.

7. Score the Innovation Game following the same procedures as in the No Problem Game in the Climate section of the Handbook Activity 3. If you choose award the winning team in some way: for example, first to line up, extra five minutes at the Game Table, etc.

Reflection: ....

The Brain Walk is a very powerful way to focus the learning experience for students. The first time you attempt this lesson, we encourage you to teach it as a "written script" or "recipe" to follow to get the most powerful thinking from your students. This activity involves all levels of thinking in the new Bloom's Revised Taxonomy, including the newest level *creativity*. It is a rigorous thinking process for both students and teachers as all stretch their thinking to blend the characteristics (attributes) to create new concepts. The spirit of collaborative competition infuses classrooms with energy and prepares students for real world experiences.

Extension: ....

This thinking activity can be used to generate ideas for:

- creative story writing, or
- science invention and design projects.

The analytical observation section of this lesson can be applied to a variety of learning experiences in different curricular areas, for example:

- studying a battle scene from a period of history, and
- eliciting characteristics of all living and non-living things before beginning an essay or written piece of work.

This would add a great deal of *Elaboration* to the final product.

NOTES

> **"All students can think. Not on the same day. Not in the same way."**
> **Kallik**

Think Tank
Living & Non-Living

2a

Living & Non-Living Category					

Name _____   Date _____

NOTE TO TEACHER: Print this as two double-sided instruments to use for Day II of the Innovation Creation activity.

Think Tank
Innovation Creation

	T	H	I	N	K
1					
2					
3					
4					
5					

Name _____   Date _____

NOTE TO TEACHER: Print this as two double-sided instruments to use for Day III of the Innovation Creation activity. Label one side "Living & Non-Living Combinations" and the other side "New Ideas."

VII Flexibility and Perception 1

Activity:	**Wordles**
Objective:	1. Students will visualize their thinking and decipher visual representations of words or phrases.
	2. Students will work with incongruities to provoke their thinking.
Strategies:	Think-Pair-Share
Elements:	Fluency, Flexibility, Originality
Fan:	Persistence
CD:	**Flexibility & Perception 1a** Wordles CD ONLY
	Flexibility & Perception 1b Wordles – Student Sample CD ONLY

Directions: ....

1. Give students a Wordles phrase and solve one together as a group (**CD Flexibility & Perception 1a).** These are visual spatial representations of words or phrases. Remember that there may be more than one "right" answer. Sometimes the positioning of a word in the box in relation to other words/symbols is part of the answer. For example: The word *man* positioned above the word *board* results in the word or phrase *man overboard*. Another example: *momanon* finds the word *man* inside the word *moon*, hence the solution *"man in the moon."*

2. Now give students the *Wordles* handout (**CD Flexibility & Perception 1a)** and give them time to solve the Wordles. Students can work individually, with a partner, or in teams (*Think-Pair-Share*). Give students as much time as they need. Do not give answers! That will ensure your students will stop thinking! (*Persistence*)

Reflection: ....

This is a powerful analytical and divergent thinking process. Students both enjoy and find high levels of challenge while participating in this activity. Some students initially will not be good at these and may even say they don't like doing these activities. Encourage students to be persistent and you will see a great leap in their skill levels in both solving and creating these challenging thinking activities. To encourage the pondering necessary for creativity you might want to have "Wordle Time" for a few minutes at the beginning of the period on a given day. Also, when students start creating Wordles, you will see their creative skills explode (*Fluency, Flexibility,* and *Originality).*

Extension: ....

Having students create some Wordles of their own to share with the class can be connected to other content learning opportunities. These can be of a general nature or may be specific to a subject or topic area. This activity can be designed as a cultural connections activity by using sayings and phrases used by people in other countries. Once created, you may give them to students one at a time on a bulletin board, document camera, etc. You can also enlarge and laminate them and create a set of "playing cards" for students to share.

ANSWERS to the Wordles handout:

1. High IQ
2. No excuse for it
3. You're under arrest
4. Courage under fire
5. Hitting below the belt
6. Man in the moon
7. Thinking out of the box
8. Short of breath or bad breath
9. Splitting headache
10. Forgive and forget
11. Raised eyebrows
12. Railroad crossing
13. No U turn
14. "The odds are against you" or "you against the odds".
15. Dirty words
16. Horseback riding

NOTES

> *"In addition to its facilitating effects in creative problem solving and creative expression, humor seems to have therapeutic effects and helps to create a healthy atmosphere in groups." Torrance*

VII Flexibility and Perception Activity 2

Activity:	**Half of Eight**
Objectives:	1. Students will learn to generate unusual solutions to problems beyond the commonly accepted "answers." 2. Students will learn to generate multiple answers and solutions once a problem has been "solved."
Strategies:	Brainstorming, Think-Pair-Share, Brain Dump, Call-back
Elements:	Fluency, Flexibility, Originality, Elaboration
Fan:	Persistence, Press, Perception
CD:	**Flexibility & Perception 2a** Half of 8 - Student Samples CD ONLY

Directions: ....

1. Ask students to get out a blank sheet of paper. Have them move to a "your brain only" spot in the classroom (*Think*). This can be anywhere they are comfortable and away from other students. Tell them you are going to ask them a question, and they are to write it in the middle of their paper. Also tell them they can ask NO questions! Ask students to write this question: "What is half of eight?" Do not spell or draw the word eight for them - simply make the statement. Give students one minute to make as many responses (*Fluency* and *Flexibility*) as they can on the paper (*Press*). At the end of the minute tell students to wad up their papers and put them on the floor beside them (*Brain Dump*). Discuss the term Brain Dump with the students, telling them they just wrote the common "easy" answers.

2. Now tell students to write the same question on the middle of another paper. Remind them to concentrate on the Rules of Brainstorming, especially rule #2 - Freewheel (*Originality*) and give them another minute to generate answers. Tell them they cannot use any of the answers from their first paper (*Persistence*). Tell students to circle their most interesting or unusual answer (*Originality*).

3. Have a bulletin board covered with paper. Call on a student, and have them draw their answer. Let them call on other students until all who want to share have posted their answers on the board (*Share*).

4. Give students 90 seconds and tell them they can use the bulletin board to Piggyback (*Press, Pair*) off of the posted answers. Tell them they are going again for more unusual answers (*Perception*). Post new answers to the bulletin board. Keep the board up for a period of time, and invite students to continue posting for a period of time (*Share*). You might want students to initial and date postings. Hopefully over time you will see more creative or elaborate examples posted. This will show students how important time and pondering are to the creative process.

Reflection: ....

Say to students, "Remember how hard it was to get your first answers? Now look at how many ideas we generated using the Think-Pair-Share technique." Now whenever you want students to generate additional options, ideas, or solutions, just use this Call-back: "What is half of 8? Start thinking - - -."

Extensions: ....

Students can explore different answers based on

- shapes,
- letters,
- foreign languages,
- mathematical concepts,
- other numbers, and
- common objects.

The possible mathematical answers are unlimited as evidenced by the following representation:

9,687,459 – 9,687,455 = 4 which is half of 8!

NOTES

> *"One key competency that employers across-the-board value in employees is the ability to think creatively and logically in order to solve problems." Partnership for 21st Century Skills*

VII Flexibility and Perception Activity 3

Activity:	**Nine Dots**
Objectives:	1. Students will work on a problem solution a number of times and learn from previous attempts and failures. 2. Students will experience the need to break down their perceptual blocks, otherwise known as "mental chains." 3. Students will practice "out-of-the-box" thinking.
Strategies:	Brainstorming, Brain Starter, Think-Pair-Share
Elements:	Fluency, Originality
Fan:	Persistence, Perception
CD:	**Flexibility & Perception 3a** Nine Dots Handout CD ONLY **Flexibility & Perception 3b** Nine Dots - Student Samples CD ONLY

Directions: ....

1. Make a copy of the *Nine Dots* handout **(CD Flexibility & Perception 3a)** and give one to each student. Give the following directions (do not add or say anything else to the basic directions):

- Connect all nine dots.
- Use no more than 4 straight lines.
- Do not lift your pencil.
- Do not retrace.

2. You can do this in a Think-Pair-Share process or use it as a Brain Starter over a period of time (*Persistence*).

Reflection: ....

This is a classic example of a perceptual block (*Perception*). We see the nine dots and imagine a square. We often even believe there are lines around the dots. These perceived lines then become fences or a boundary we believe we cannot cross. This perceptual block prevents us from obtaining a solution. Should a student get a solution quickly, challenge them to arrive at another solution (*Fluency*). Do not give the students the answer! Give students the opportunity to work for weeks on this problem as well as challenge them to generate additional answers (*Persistence*)!

Extensions: ....

Collect various solutions from students over time to create a portfolio of their work to share. Here are two classic answers to this activity:

Emphasize with students that by extending the line and "breaking the boundaries" or "mental chains" we put on our thinking (perceptual blocks), we can arrive at a solution. Additional very original answers include:

- Go through all 9 dots with the stroke of a very thick marker (one line).
- Cut the paper into three strips, lay the strips end-to-end, and go through all nine dots with one line.
- Fold the paper to form a sphere and then go through all nine dots with three lines.
- There are as many as *25 solutions* to this classic problem!
- Student generated samples are included in this activity.

<u>NOTES</u>

"As competition intensifies, so does the need for creative thinking. It is no longer enough to do the same thing better. It is no longer enough to be efficient and to solve problems. Far more is needed." de Bono

VII Flexibility and Perception 4

Activity:	**Brain Riddles**
Objective:	Students will use both convergent and divergent thinking skills simultaneously to solve the brain riddles.
Strategies:	Think-Pair-Share, Anchoring, Brain Starter
Elements:	Flexibility, Originality
Fan:	Persistence, Perception
CD:	**Flexibility & Perception 4a** Classic Brain Riddles CD ONLY

Directions: ....

1. Give students the handout of Sample *Classic Brain Riddles* **(CD Flexibility & Perception 4a)**. Let them work individually or with a partner (*Think-Pair-Share*). Once they have worked for 10 – 15 minutes, have them put the handout away.

2. Revisit the handout in a day or two. You can use these Brain Riddles as an anchoring activity or on-going Brain Starter. Let students work on them:

   - when they first enter your room,
   - at the beginning of class,
   - when they have finished their work, or
   - any time you want during a period of instruction.

3. Let students *struggle* (*Persistence*) with these for three or four weeks (or more). A list of 20 has been provided; however, you can go on-line and search *riddles, brain riddles, logic puzzles*, etc., to get many more.

Reflection: ....

A benefit of the Brain Riddles is that, for most students, there may be more than one *"right"* answer. Look at the riddles provided. Sometimes a second or third possible answer may be presented in the parentheses. Accept answers from students when they can logically and creatively explain their answers. Think of all the processes your students will be using as they attempt to solve these riddles:

   - trial & error,
   - complex analytical thought, and
   - manipulating language (creating puns).

This is an activity where the students are required to do almost simultaneous convergent and divergent thinking. It is a very intense process and is best scheduled over a long period of time or at different intervals throughout the curriculum.

A favorite quotation about thinking is the following: "How do you get a student to stop thinking? Give her the answer!" Every time we rush to get "closure" on a question, topic, or a unit of study, we rob students not only of the *struggle* (*Persistence*) that accompanies most worthwhile and rigorous work but the sense of *accomplishment* and resulting celebration of success. Every time we give students the answer, we send a subliminal message unintentionally, "You can't do this. You are not capable. So I will have to help you or tell you." Let them *wrestle* (*Persistence*) with the work!

Extension: ....

Teachers are encouraged to create a collection of riddles that require students to process intensely to resolve them. Students will also bring you riddles from a variety of sources to add to your collection. Students also enjoy the challenge of creating their own riddles.

Classic Brain Riddles Answers

1. a towel	11. a glove
2. a cold	12. nothing
3. a hole	13. suicide
4. the letter E	14. a coffin
5. counterfeit money	15. tomorrow
6. the word "wholesome"	16. time
7. trust	17. a snail
8. corn on the cob	18. stars (dreams)
9. a sponge	19. a dictionary
10. a nose	20. an eye

NOTES

"Not everything that counts can be counted, and not everything that can be counted counts." Einstein

VII Flexibility and Perception Activity 5

Activity:	**Creative Math**
Objective:	1. Students will explore changing their perceptions to solve creative math problems.
Strategies:	Think-Pair-Share
Elements:	Originality
Fan:	Perception, Press
CD:	**Flexibility & Perception 5a** Creative Math Test CD ONLY
	Flexibility & Perception 5b Creative Numbers CD ONLY
	Flexibility & Perception 5c Balancing Creative Math Problem CD ONLY

Directions: Creative Math Test ....

1.   Begin by giving a copy of the *Creative Math Test* handout to each student. **(CD Flexibility & Perception 5a).** *NOTE: This example is for middle or high school students. Teachers can easily create an elementary version.* Explain that this will be a timed test (*Press*) to determine their math ability. Tell students they are to *find the three false statements*. Underline or circle each one.

2.   Explain that they will need to work quickly as they will only have *three minutes.(Press)*

3.   As students attempt this activity, most will begin by working the solution to number 1 and then move in order through the seven problems. If they solve the problems correctly, they will soon find *only two* are incorrect. Usually, if they have enough time, they will then begin to recheck their work, looking for another incorrect answer. All work will stay within the seven-presented problems, because they have considered this a math exercise.

4.   In the Math Test, number 2 is incorrect (the correct answer is 81) and number 3 is incorrect (the correct answer is 108). As the students work out the answers to 1, 4, 5, 6, & 7 they will discover that they are all correct! Therefore, the third false statement is, "There are *three* false statements here." In fact, there are only *two* false statements here!

Directions: Creative Numbers ....

1.   Distribute a copy of the *Creative Numbers* activity to each student **(CD Flexibility & Perception 5b).**

2.   Ask students, "Which of the following numbers is most different from the others?" Tell them this is a "Your Brain Only" activity for 15 seconds (*Press*). Then ask them to get a partner, and compare their answers for another 60 seconds. Students will explain their choices and reasoning to each other.

3. Now tell students that before hearing their answers, you would like to tell them *your answer*. Say, "I think the answer is "2" because it is the only *even* number – the rest are odd numbers!"

4. Students will argue that '2' was not one of the choices. Their perceptual blocks (*Perception*) are working well! When they look at that problem, they believe the only possible answers come from the choices "three," "thirteen," and "thirty-one." Interestingly, those choices *are not even in numerical form (numbers)*!

Directions: Balancing Creative Math ....

1. Give each student the handout *Balancing Creative Math Problem* **(CD Flexibility & Perception 5c)**.

2. Allow them to work individually and then with a partner (*Think-Pair-Share*).

3. The Balancing Creative Math Problem can be solved by leaving out one coin and putting two coins on each side of the balance. If the two sides balance, the coin not being weighed is the correct one. If one side is heavier or lighter, an additional weighing can solve the problem.

Reflection: ....

1. First, it is important for students to understand that we need creative thinking in *all subject areas*. Secondly, you probably saw your students' perceptual blocks (*Perception*) getting in the way of their thinking about these creative challenges. In math, you may find your students jumping right to the perceived *computation* or *calculation* of a problem without looking at all the information provided or what the question is really asking.

2. Each of these activities stimulate student thinking in different manners and are intended to be done during separate time periods so students will focus only on the type of challenge in each one.

Extension: ....

There are many resources teachers can find to begin a collection of these types of math problems. Additionally, students are also good at generating their own after they have worked with these types of problems.

<u>NOTES</u>

> *"Online gaming can help students develop many of the skills they'll be required to use upon leaving school, such as critical thinking, problem solving, and creativity." Devaney*

VII Flexibility and Perception Activity 6

Activity:	**Minute Mysteries**
Objectives:	1. Students will generate questions and use trial and error to obtain the correct answers. 2. Students will practice changing their preconceived ideas and perceptions through questioning.
Strategies:	Questioning, Trial & Error
Elements:	Fluency, Flexibility, Originality, Elaboration
Fan:	Persistence, Perception, Process
CD:	**Flexibility & Perception 6a** Minute Mystery Data Form CD ONLY

Directions: ....

1. Give each student a copy of the *Minute Mystery* handout **(CD Flexibility & Perception 6a)**.

2. Tell students they are going to try to solve a mystery by asking questions to get clues. With each clue they will build a possible solution (*trial and error*). Process the following Minute Mystery together as an example:

3. "This Minute Mystery is called *The Chess Players*. I will read it to you. You will then be able to ask me questions that can only be answered with a "Yes" or a "No."
Minute Mystery: "Two girls were playing chess. They played five games and they each won three. How is this possible?"

4. You can do this activity until a solution is reached (usually in 15 to 30 minutes). Alternately, you may allow students to come to you throughout the class period (or even the entire day) for a "yes" or "no" answer to a question they have written. As students continue to get answers to their questions (Persistence), they begin to build guesses and speculations (trial and error) as to the solution to the mystery posed.

5. Cut and paste additional mysteries on the Minute Mystery Handout.

Reflection: ....

Formulating and asking specific questions is a valuable life skill. Forcing the questions into a 'Yes" or "No" format can be an even more valuable skill. As students begin to formulate possible solutions, they must speculate and often "think outside the box" by changing their Perceptions. It is important to give students these one at a time to keep them focused on being persistent with the task.

Extension: ....

This activity also works well as a small group or whole class activity. Read the mystery and then allow students to ask questions. When processed as a whole class activity students can build upon the questions of classmates (*Piggybacking*) as they move toward a solution (*Process*). If you choose to have students *process* this activity in small groups, one student can be the person who answers the questions. Students will also enjoy the challenge of creating their own Minute Mysteries.

Answers to Minute Mysteries

> **Minute Mystery: Chess Players**
> (The girls played other players, not each other.)
> **Minute Mystery: Dentist**
> (The dentist was the boy's Mother.)
> **Minute Mystery: Time Traveller**
> (The name of the man's horse was *Thursday*.)
> **Minute Mystery: The New Suit**
> (The man was an astronaut – or deep-sea diver.)
> **Minute Mystery: John and Mary**
> (John and Mary were goldfish.)
> **Minute Mystery: The Pack Man**
> (The man's parachute failed to open.)

Minute Mysteries to Cut and Paste onto the Data Form

Minute Mystery: Dentist

"A boy went to the dentist for a check-up. The boy was the dentist's son, but the dentist was not the boy's father. How can this be?"

Minute Mystery: Time Traveller

"A man rode into the town on Thursday. He stayed in the town for three days. Then he left town on Thursday. How is this possible?"

Minute Mystery: The New Suit

"A man went to work wearing a new suit. While working he developed a small tear in the sleeve. A minute later he was dead. How is this possible?"

Minute Mystery: John and Mary

"John and Mary were dead on the floor. Next to them was a small puddle of water and pieces of broken glass. How did they die?"

Minute Mystery: The Pack Man

"A man was found dead in a field with a pack on his back. How did he die?"

VII Flexibility and Perception Activity 7

Activity:	**Create a Code**
Objective:	Students will practice and expand their convergent and divergent thinking by "cracking" or creating codes.
Strategies:	Trial and Error
Elements:	Fluency, Flexibility, Originality
Fan:	Persistence, Product, Process, Passion
CD:	**Flexibility & Perception 7a** Create a Code CD ONLY **Flexibility & Perception 7b** Message Codes CD ONLY **Flexibility & Perception 7c** Code Combos CD ONLY

Directions: ....

1. Begin by discussing with your students the meaning of the following words:
   - Communication - it takes place when there is a sender, a means of transmission, and a receiver.
   - Language - it is created when meaning is given to symbols, letters, words, and gestures.

2. Next ask students, "What is a code?" Codes are created when we substitute an unfamiliar or new set of symbols for familiar ones.

3. Present the example of the numbers 1, 2, and 3. They form a recognizable pattern. However, if we substitute # for 1, * for 2, and @ for 3, then the number 13 would now be written as #@.

4. To figure out or decipher a code, you must first determine what each new symbol means and then translate the coded message back into one with which you are familiar. Let's begin by deciphering an easy number code.

5. Distribute a copy of the *Create a Code* handout **(CD Flexibility & Perception 7a)** to each student. Allow them time to crack the code *(Process)*.

6. You may follow-up with the *Message Codes* **(CD Flexibility & Perception 7b)** and the *Code Combos* handouts **(CD Flexibility & Perception 7c)**. You may use these over a period of several days or longer *(Persistence)* which may result in some students developing a *passion* in this area. The codes activities and extensions are also excellent *anchoring activities!*

Reflection: ....

Children have always been fascinated by the idea of a secret code. Not only can they use their *imagination* (*Fluency, Flexibility,* and *Originality*) when thinking about codes, but they can also employ the higher-level thinking skills of *analysis, synthesis, and creating* when creating and solving them (*Product*).

Extension: ....

1. Refer to the code variations on the handouts.

2. In the following line of letters, cross out six letters so the remaining letters, without altering the sequence, will spell a familiar word.

B S A I N X L E A T N T E A R S = (banana)

(Adapted from von Oech (1998) A Whack on the Side of the Head)

When you cross out the words *six letters*, what is left is the word *banana*! Of course, most of us try to cross out 6 letters (*Perception*).

3. Which of the following letters do you perceive to be the odd one out?

T P H E M

Answer: Each letter can be supported as being the odd one out. For example, P is the only letter with a curved line. E is the only vowel. See how many ways your students can support their letter as the odd one out.

NOTES

"Le hasard favorise l'esprit prepare" – "Chance favors the prepared mind." Louis Pasteur

VIII Animation Unit

Overview: Students will work in a long-term, product-based unit to build skills for 21st century learning. These skills include: creative thinking, critical thinking, problem solving, collaboration, and communication.

Curriculum Standards Connections: This unit, with its activities and extensions, may be designed to have strong curricular connections. It is a unit on creativity that allows you to integrate all content areas.

Elements: Fluency, Flexibility, Originality, Elaboration

Fan: Person, Persistence, Process, Product, Press, Perception, and Passion

Summary:

Curriculum Integration

This unit is comprised of many components with steps and procedures that can be used in flexible time formats. The complete unit incorporates a variety of technology tools and areas of skill development. Learning that involves animations associated with in-depth content explorations produce both K.M.S.☺. student products and rigorous learning experiences. Here are some content-related animation product examples that have been created by students:

Thaumatropes:

Salem Witch Burning (U.S. History)   Alexander the Great (World History)

Flip Books:

DNA Helix (Science)   No Smoking (Health)

Animations:

Rainforest (Social Studies)   Continents (Geography)

A curricular area of study can be carried throughout each individual product leading to the final animation product. For example: a student could start out with a thaumatrope representing the Salem Witch burnings, carry that content theme through a flip book, and culminate with several different animation products using different media. The following is a list of the sequential activities that culminate in a long-term animation product.

Animation 1: Tech Talk   **Animation 4:** Flip books
Animation 2: Thaumatropes   **Animation 5:** "Bendy Guy"
Animation 3: Draw Starts   **Animation 6:** Final Animations:
                                                      a. Paper-Cut-Outs b. Coin
                                                      c. Chalk   or   d. Clay

Technology & Creativity Skill Development

All animations are created using stop-motion animation. This is an animation process that involves students:

  a. creating characters and backgrounds

  b. taking a series of pictures with a digital camera of incremental character movements (similar to character movements on their flip books)

  c. putting the photos into a computer program that allows for editing, such as Flash MX or IMovie.

Stop-motion animation provides students with a rich learning experience. They will actually create the animated techniques by the placement and design of the characters and objects in their animations. This is a complex creative and thinking assignment for students that challenges them more rigorously than simply using pre-programmed animation technology.

Visual Spatial Learning

Visual representations of thinking are powerful learning processes that can improve students' ability to demonstrate their thinking and understanding of material presented. This is especially true for students who have difficulty processing information in a written or verbal format. They may excel when given an opportunity to use visual representations to demonstrate their learning. With today's Web 2.0 tools at your fingertips, these products can range from very intensive processes like stop animation using a FLASH MX, to quicker, simpler processes using programs like IMovie.

Fluid Differentiation

Students may work through a series of products at their own rate. This flexibility, inherent in product-based learning, allows the teacher to set levels of rigor for different individuals. This is an effective, yet somewhat simplified, version of differentiation (Fluid Differentiation). Once this type of organization is in place, differentiation becomes seamless, as all students are working on various stages of their animations and skill development. The "individual product structure" allows teachers to work with individuals and small groups as needed to differentiate instruction (for core content instruction), while the whole group moves in and out of animation product work. Students are also given the opportunity to work outside the classroom if they choose. Some students need this extra time just to stay up with the required output, while others will choose to use the extra time to work towards K.M.S.☺.

Animation Lesson 1: Animation Tech Talk

Objective: Students will understand the skills and techniques of animation.

Elements: Fluency

Fan: Perception, Process

CD: **1a** Animation Tech Talk Terms
1b Animation Tech Talk Log
1c Animation Tech Talk Quiz

Directions: ....

1. Give each student the **Tech Talk Terms** handout **(Animation 1a)**. Tell them to silently read the definitions and complete the tasks listed on the handout.

2. Ask for volunteers to explain what they think (*Perception*) is happening when they completed the persistence of vision activity. This is a good time to use the feedback of cold, warm, and hot to guide students towards the correct explanation. Here are some discussion/comments to include:

   • How many fingers did you see and why? What happened if you slowed down the finger shake?

   • What do you think is happening inside your brain to cause the blurred/multiple fingers to appear?

   • After allowing students a variety of explanations, tell them the brain "holds an image" for a short while. If you introduce another image quickly, the second image is there with the first image. This is why they see many fingers when they shake them rapidly.

3. Ask students if they have seen the old reels of film that were used to show moving pictures (films), or possibly home movies, many years earlier? If possible, bring some film in to show students.

4. Before giving the samples to students, ask them (in a very serious voice), "Are the tiny people and objects moving around on the film?" It is interesting to note that in most classes you will have some students initially say, "Yes", and then think again, laugh, and quickly and say, "No" which then emotionally connects them to this learning concept.

5. Pose the next question, "How do we use film to show motion?" Tell them to get with a partner and explain how they believe this Process works. Now ask for ideas and discuss the concept of *persistence of vision* as it applies to showing a film.

6. Share with students that approximately 24 frames per second must move across the viewing space to create motion. Any noticeable decrease or increase would affect the projected image. Ask them how they think the change in speed would affect the image (blurry, jumpy, etc.).

7. Now show the class a series of classic cartoons and ask them to complete the Animation Tech Talk Log **(Animation 1b)**. Tell students to keep this sheet and study the terms as they will have a Tech Talk Quiz **(Animation 1c)** in the near future on Tech Terms. Discuss each of the Tech Terms as a class and ask students to also share as many examples they can quickly think of (Fluency) from some of their favorite movies or cartoons.

8. Give students the Animation Tech Talk Quiz **(Animation 1c)**.

Reflection: ....

This lesson introduces students to the terminology they will need to know and use when they begin animation activities. It is interesting to see students leap from the "magic" they first believe is happening on film to the analytical process of *persistence of vision.*

Below are classic cartoons I used for the Tech Terms Log activity:

1. Looney Toons: Road Runner

2. Disney Classics: Mickey Mouse, Donald Duck, Elmer Fudd

3. Warner Brothers: Sylvester and Tweety

4. Hanna and Barbera: Tom and Jerry

Extension:...

Over a period of time your students could create a graffiti wall of animation techniques they observe in movies or cartoons.

Answer Key: Animation Tech Talk Quiz

<u>6</u>   Secondary Action

<u>1</u>   Squash & Stretch

<u>4</u>   Staging

<u>9</u>   Character Analysis

<u>3</u>   Follow Through and Overlapping Action

<u>5</u>   Slow In & Slow Out or Fast In & Fast Out

<u>7</u>   Exaggeration

<u>2</u>   Anticipation

<u>8</u>   Paths of Movement

<u>10</u> Foreshadowing

1a

Animation Tech Talk Terms

Name _____   Date_____

1. SQUASH & STRETCH – distorts (stretches) a shape to accent the movement.

2. ANTICIPATION – a reverse movement or pause to accent a forward move.

3. FOLLOW THROUGH AND OVERLAPPING ACTION – nothing stops abruptly - all movement is very, very smooth.

4. STAGING – placing the camera at different angles or viewpoints to get the best shot affect (weird angles, zooming in or out, poses, shooting through openings, etc.).

5. SLOW IN & SLOW OUT or FAST IN & FAST OUT – changing the speed of the camera action or character movement to emphasize a moment.

6. SECONDARY ACTIONS – having a main movement along with an additional movement of less importance.

7. EXAGGERATION – caricatures or distortions of actions OR designs that poke fun of someone or something.

8. PATHS OF MOVEMENT – a purposeful planned action or movement (circles – scallops -loops, zigzags, - etc.).

9. CHARACTER ANALYSIS – what the character or animated item is portraying. What emotion do they bring? What is their purpose in the story? Is this usually considered a traditional or classic stereotypical character role?

10. FORESHADOWING – an action or visual in a film that pre-stages (shows or hints at) what will happen much later in the film.

PERSISTENCE OF VISION: Shake your hand up and down rapidly with your fingers extended. How many fingers do you see? _____? Try shaking your hand faster or slower. What happens to the image? Record what you think is happening in your brain as you view your fingers.

1b   # Animation Tech Talk Log

Students: As you watch the classic cartoons, write down the examples of each of the tech terms below. Use this handout to study for the Tech Terms Test.

TECH TERMS	DEFINITIONS	CARTOON/ MOVIE EXAMPLES
SQUASH & STRETCH		
ANTICIPATION		
FOLLOW THROUGH/ OVERLAPPING ACTION		
STAGING		
SLOW IN & SLOW OUT FAST IN & FAST OUT		
SECONDARY ACTIONS		
EXAGGERATION		
PATHS OF MOVEMENT		
CHARACTER ANALYSIS		
FORESHADOWING		
OTHER IDEAS		

Animation Tech Talk Quiz

1c

Name _____ Date_____ _____ /15 points

1. Distorting and/or stretching a shape to accent the movement.
2. A reverse movement or pause to accent a forward move.
3. All movement is very smooth and does not stop abruptly.
4. Placing the camera at different angles or viewpoints.
5. Changing the speed of the camera action or character movement.
6. Having a movement in the background of the animation.
7. Caricatures/exaggerations of actions OR events in the animation.
8. Purposefully planning circles, scallops, loop, zigzags, etc. into the animation.
9. Classical or stereotypical character being portrayed in the animation.
10. "Hinting" with words or pictures at something that is going to happen later in the film.

_____

Put the correct number of the definition for each term below.

_____ SECONDARY ACTIONS　　　　_____ EXAGGERATION

_____ SQUASH & STRETCH　　　　　_____ ANTICIPATION

_____ STAGING　　　　　　　　　　_____ PATHS OF MOVEMENT

_____ CHARACTER ANALYSIS　　　　_____ FORESHADOWING

_____ FOLLOW THROUGH AND OVERLAPPING ACTION

_____ SLOW IN & SLOW OUT or FAST IN & FAST OUT

ON THE BACK:

1. Write your definition of **PERSISTENCE OF VISION**: (3 or more thoughts)

2. Select three of the animation techniques and give detailed examples for each from a cartoon or movie you have seen.

> **Animation Lesson 2:   Thaumatrope Animation**
>
> **Objective:**   Students will create a product that produces *persistence of vision* to further understand the concept.
>
> **Strategies:**   Brain Walk
>
> **Elements:**   Originality, Elaboration
>
> **Fan:**   Process, Product
>
> **CD:**   **2a** Thaumatrope Templates CD ONLY
> **2b** Thaumatrope - Student Samples (6) CD ONLY

Directions (Part I): Introducing Thaumatropes...

1. Students must complete the Tech Talk Animation lesson before introducing this lesson.

2. Begin this lesson with a Brain Walk *(Process)*. If you do not have prior students' products, you can find or create samples with clip art taped to paper plates until you begin your student product portfolio **(Animation 2a).**

3. Tell each student to pick up a thaumatrope and to wind up the rubber bands until they are tightly wound. Release the plate so the thaumatrope twirls between their hands to test the samples.

4. At the end of the Brain Walk have students select a favorite thaumatrope and join you in a group to discuss and evaluate the products. It is helpful to have examples of some products that don't work well to better help students understand what works best. Discuss with students what they notice works best as they demonstrate their selection to the other students and tell why they chose that particular product. Their observations should include:

- Objects are drawn neatly.
- Objects are correctly placed (one is upside down and one is right side up).
- Objects are outlined in a dark color (so they are clear on rotation).
- Objects are large enough to be clearly seen.

Directions (Part II): Designing a Thamatrope ....

5. Cut out the large center circles on two uncoated plain paper plates. Punch holes on opposite sides of each plate (not too close to the edge) to prevent tearing of the holes. Insert a thick rubber band into each hole and put one end of the rubber band through the open loop of the rubber band and pull to tighten securely to the plate. The steps to complete the Thaumatrope *(Product)* are:

- Find design ideas in magazines or on the computer.
- Draw your design drafts on pieces of paper.
- Tape drafts onto each thaumatrope paper plate circle to determine positioning.
- Practice twirling thaumatropes to check for animation. Reposition as needed.

- Pencil draft designs on to the paper plates. Make drawings as large as possible so they can be easily seen in "action."
- See the teacher for approval of the design and position of the animated parts.
- Take off the rubber bands and separate the paper plates. Add color to your designs while the plates are separated to prevent color bleeding through plates.
- Outline thaumatropes in dark colors to further emphasize designs.
- Add Elaboration (details) as time permits – see teacher for suggestions to K.M.S.☺.

NOTE: See student samples **(Animation 2b):** Monkey and Flag, Friends and Aliens, and Face and Spider.

Reflection: ....

Thaumatrope comes from two Greek words meaning "turning marvel" and it was invented by John Paris in 1825. When students are successful at creating a thaumatrope it helps them fully understand the meaning of the tech term *persistence of vision* (Process). This is also one of the basic animation lessons that allows you to help students focus on using clip art ideas from computers and magazines and turning them into their own "original" designs.

Extension: ....

The subject matter for the thaumatrope can be linked to all content areas.

(Example)

2a

Thaumatrope Templates

Animation Lesson 3: Draw Starts	
Objective:	Students will learn and practice basic cartoon drawing skills that they can use in animation projects.
Strategies:	Brain Walk, Piggyback
Elements:	Originality, Elaboration
Fan:	Perception
CD:	**3a** Draw Starts Guide
	3b Draw Starts Characters CD ONLY
	3c Draw Starts - Student Samples (1 and 2) CD ONLY

Directions: ....

1. Provide students with a blank *Draw Starts Character* handout (**Animation 3b**) printed double-sided.

2. Demonstrate the three basic face positioning of features while students draw along with you (mimicking each stroke). See the *Draw Starts Guide* handout **(Animation 3a)** for your reference (the cross of the lines is where the nose goes).

3. Draw each individually and give students time to come up with their own creative versions (*Fluency* and *Elaboration*) by adding different shaped eyes, ears, mouths, hair designs, etc. (*Perception*). See the *student sample Draw Starts* **(Animation 3c)** for ideas.

4. Have students do a Brain Walk about half way through the activity to Piggyback off of ideas of others.

Reflection: ....

Students really enjoy this activity and are amazed at how fast their animated drawing skills can develop.

Extension: ....

Students can use the same techniques on inanimate objects. All these types of drawings can be used in flip books and in chalk animations.

NOTES

3a

Draw Starts Guide

Draw the eyes and the nose near the cross of guidelines to get the desired effect of positioning the viewing direction of the character. Guidelines and the draft drawings are to be done lightly in pencil so changes can be erased.

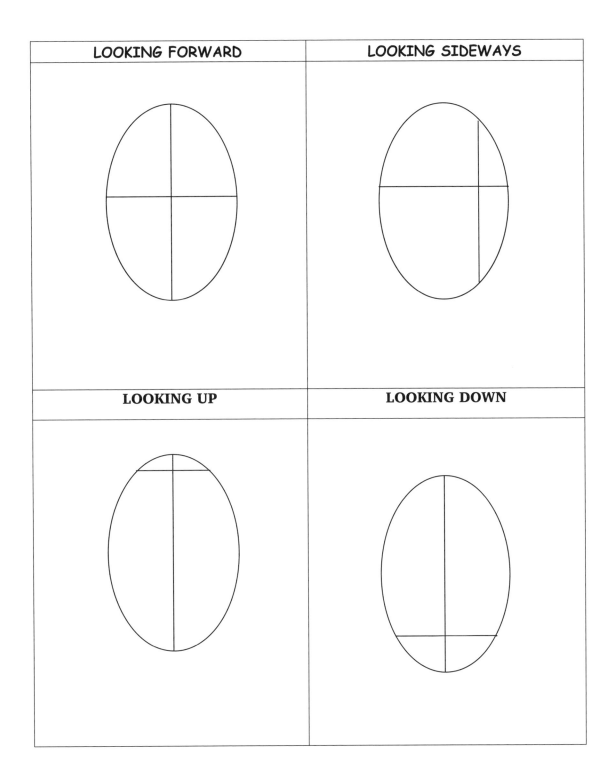

LOOKING FORWARD	LOOKING SIDEWAYS
LOOKING UP	**LOOKING DOWN**

Animation Lesson 4: Flip Books

Objective:	1. Students will understand how to create different patterns of animated movement.
	2. Students will practice the thinking and planning required to make animation happen.
	3. Students will practice and understand the power of "backwards planning."
Strategies:	Brain Walk, Anchoring
Elements:	Originality, Elaboration
Fan:	Persistence, Product
CD:	**4a** Animation Elaboration Log
	4b Flip Tips
	4c Flip Book Animation Patterns of Movement
	4d Flip Book Animation Plan
	4e Flip Book - Student Samples CD ONLY

Directions (Part I): Elaboration Log ....

1. Discuss the Elaboration element of creativity as it applies to character and/or scenery detail design and to the detailed movement of characters or objects.

2. Show the students some animation videos and have them record examples of Elaboration (movement and character design) on the *Animation Elaboration Log* handout **(Animation 4a)**.

3. After the video screening, discuss details the students discovered. The goal for the students is to record five or more items in each column of the log. Suggested animation videos: Martin the Cobbler, Rip Van Winkle, and the Little Prince from Will Vinton Studio Productions (my favorites)!

4. Discuss with students how they might use Elaboration in their flip books and future animation products.

5. Ask students how Elaboration can be used to improve written assignments.

Directions (Part II): ....

1. Show students some on-line samples of flip books (Google flip books). Watch the flip books on a large screen projection system if possible or have students grouped at several computers to discuss the tech terms they see occurring in the actions.

2. Discuss animation techniques with the students. *Squash and stretch* is a favorite technique used in many flip books. A second favorite technique is *staging,* where an item or object keeps getting bigger and bigger, and sometimes you only see a part of the item as the close-up continues to move into view. This would also be a good time to discuss how important one tech term, *patterns of movement,* is in designing the flip books. Have the students notice some of the following *Patterns of Movement* **(Animation 4c):**

- *Center break-apart* - an item or object is in the center of the page and it breaks apart and moves out towards the four corners.

- *Move to center* - parts of an item or object are drawn in each corner of the page and, on progressive pages, the items move towards the center to make an item or object.

- *Simple movement plans* - up and down, right to left, left to right, zigzags, roller coaster, twirl, etc.

- *Pop ins and outs* - a complete item or object is totally drawn on a page, may stay for a few pages, and then just quickly disappears.

- *Build on to or take aparts* - this is one of the simpler techniques for flip books as objects don't necessarily need to have movement patterns. It can be as simple as starting a drawing of a face (kind of line by line) until at the end of the flip book you see the entire face. This process can also be reversed. These types of plans are good for items like fruit bowls, anatomy parts (e.g. parts of the brain), building a skyline, etc.

3. Students can also print out mini flip books and staple them to observe some of these techniques. The teacher can also provide a set of professional flip books for this review.

4. Have students complete a Brain Walk of student products or professional flip books and select the one that K.M.S.☺. and then join the discussion circle at the front of the room to evaluate the products.

5. Pass out the *Flip Tips* **(Animation 4b)** and review together before students complete their *Flip Book Animation Plan* sheet **(Animation 4d)**.

6. Review the Flip Book Animation Planning sheet with students.

7. Pass out twenty-five 3 x 5 index cards to each student after their planning sheet has been approved by the teacher.

8. Flip books are great projects to keep in the classroom as anchoring activities that can be worked on over a long period of time at short or medium intervals in several class periods. The flip books should only be released for independent work outside of the classroom after the teacher has approved it as a final draft stage. This stage is achieved only when the teacher initials the flip book as meeting all the planning sheet requirements and determines that it is ready for the student to add color and more elaborate details. Flip books are the type of learning activity that helps students see the value in both the skills of patience and persistence and their relationship to quality work.

9. Have a final celebration presentation of the flip books with a Brain Walk and sharing of the final products.

Reflection: ....

Improving visual thinking helps students in other types of learning opportunities they will experience in other content areas. For some students, if they can visualize their learning concept, it will help them assimilate new concepts and patterns.

Flip books are the type of engaging products that can be used to get students to produce quality work. Remind students that this product does not require good drawing skills, as they can trace clip art or drawings to create the initial pattern for their item or object. Students are required to add Elaboration to the clip art to make their own original items or objects for their animation. Successful flip books are more a result of thinking and planning and careful Persistent work.

Extension: ....
The content of the flip book can be connected to any curricular area of study.

Animation Elaboration Log (Details)

4a

Name_____ Date_____

LITTLE PRINCE	MARTIN COBBLER	RIP VAN W.
MOVEMENT	MOVEMENT	MOVEMENT
VISUAL	VISUAL	VISUAL

Directions: As you watch the Claymation DVD record examples of detailed movements and visual details (goal of 5 or more in each column) in characters of scenery.

4b   # Flip Tips

1. Start thinking about your character design. Gather ideas from clipart, magazines, etc. Remember you can trace these to make patterns for your flip book. But you must piggyback off of the clip art and create your own version.

2. Decide how your characters or objects would fit best on your flip book. Horizontal? Vertical? Think about the paths of movement that will occur, the shape of your characters, and objects to help you make this decision.

3. Keep your drawings simple as you will possibly be drawing them many times to complete your flip book. You can always go back and add details if time permits and you are trying to get K.M.S.☺. points. Make a pattern to trace once you have created your characters or objects.

4. Draw your completed last page before you begin your flip book. Now you know what you are going to complete before you begin the flip book. It is recommended that you work forward from your last page (backwards design). If you are not comfortable with this, you can start from the beginning, but you must have the last page completed before starting the beginning pages.

5. Remember to draw your entire scene only on the last 2/3 of your index card. If you draw too close to the flipping side you will not be able to see the drawings as you flip the flip book. Move each character or object only about 1/8 inch on each page to keep your movement smooth.

6. Draft all drawings in pencil and remember you can take out and add index cards as needed. Keep your index cards together with a rubber band.

7. Flip your flip book frequently to see if you are accomplishing your actions clearly and at the speed that you want them to happen.

8. Remember to go step-by-step through the planning steps and get them initialed before proceeding to the next step. Do not get in a hurry; this is a long-term in- class project. You may work outside of class once your draft is approved.

4c　　　　　**Flip Book Animation Patterns of Movement**

- *Center break-apart* - an item or object is in the center of the page and it breaks apart and moves out towards the four corners.

- *Move to center* - parts of an item or object are drawn in each corner of the page and, on progressive pages, the items move towards the center to make an item or object.

- *Simple movement plans* - up and down, right to left, left to right, zigzags, roller coaster, twirl, etc.

- *Pop ins and outs* - a complete item or object is totally drawn on a page, may stay for a few pages, and then just quickly disappears.

- *Build on to or take aparts* - this is one of the simpler techniques for flip books as objects don't necessarily need to have movement patterns. It can be as simple as starting a drawing of a face (kind of line by line) until at the end of the flip book you see the entire face. This process can also be reversed. These types of plans are good for items like fruit bowls, anatomy parts (e.g. parts of the brain), building a skyline, etc.

4d

Flip Book Animation Plan

Name _____ Date _____

1. The animation techniques I used are:

    a. Path of Movement_____ (__/5pts.)

    b. Other_____ (__/5pts.)

2. My statement of action is _____ (__/5pts.)

3. My flip book will be designed _____ Horizontal _____ Vertical

4. I have completed the Action Steps and Draft Designs on the back of this page.

5. Planning steps: initial each as you finish each step. Bring these items to the teacher and get each part initialed/approved as you complete the requirements. You must have each one initialed/approved before going on to the next requirement.

    ____ I have completed the planning sheet (front and back) and picked up 25 index cards and a rubber band. Write your name and class on the back card.

    ____ I have drawn the completed last page of my flip book.

    ____ I have a draft of the first ten pages.

    ____ I have included a character, object/item, and background.

    ____ I have competed the draft of all 25 pages.

    ____ I have had 3 individual conferences with other students and they have added written suggestions and their initials to the back of my flip book.

    ____ I have added elaboration details of movement and design after having an "ideas conference" with 3 other students. Things I added:

        _____

    _____

    ____ I have added elaboration details of movement and design after having an "ideas Conference" with my teacher. Things I added:

        _____

    _____

    ____ I have added color to my flip book.

    ____ I have designed a unique and "eye-catching" cover card for my flip book.

    ____ I have designed a detailed and unique credits page card.

    ____ I have outlined my flip book with a bold (usually black) marker to make my character, object/item, and background show up clearly.

Complete the back of this sheet before conferencing with you teacher.　　All Initials (__/5pts.)

Directions: Sketch and describe the details of design and movement you are planning to use.	
DESIGN ELABORATIONS Details added to designs (neatness counts)!	**MOVEMENT ELABORATIONS** Detailed movements are clearly seen!
(____/5pts.)	Details of beginning movements: (5 or more) (____/5pts.)
(____/5pts.)	Details of middle movements: (5 or more) (____/5pts.)
(____/5pts.)	Details of ending movements: (5 or more) (____/5pts.)

APPROVED BY _____ (teacher) DATE_____

Your total points will be given by your teacher when you turn in the final project.

Total_____/50

Animation Lesson 5: Bendy Guy

Objective: 1. Students will create a "Bendy Guy" animation product to demonstrate they can execute all Tech Terms (see Tech Terms Activity) correctly.

2. Students will learn how to use a camera and a computer program to produce a "Bendy Guy" animation.

Strategies: Animation Tech Terms
Elements: Fluency, Flexibility, Originality
Fan: Process
CD: **5a** Bendy Guy Plan – Technical Practice Animation
                   5b Animation Tech Talk
                   5c Bendy Guy Mini Storyboard
                   5d Camera Introduction & Safety CD ONLY
                   5e Bendy Guy Animation Photos – Student Samples CD ONLY

Directions: ....

This is an introductory-level animation lesson involving no character or background design. Students can use a piece of construction paper, desk top, carpet, etc. as the background.

1. Demonstrate camera safety and handling and give students the *Camera Introduction & Safety* handout **(Animation 5d).** You may edit this one to fit your needs.

2. Demonstrate how to use the animation program you have selected.

3. Review and discuss *the Bendy Guy Plan* **(Animation 5a)** and *Bendy Guy Mini Storyboard* **(Animation 5c)** handouts.

4. Have mini-conferences with students as needed to complete the Bendy Guy task list and for feedback and support as students complete their animations.

5. Schedule Bendy Guy presentation days and use the Bendy Guy plan to evaluate the animation.

Reflection: ....

One goal of this activity is to familiarize students with a mini-planning procedure for an animation and to teach them all the technical skills they will need to create any level of stop-action animation. Even though this animation requires a minimal plan, students will be able to use the Elements of Fluency, Flexibility, and Originality in the design of their Bendy Guy story. When evaluating the Bendy Guy Animation, it is important to assess that students have clearly demonstrated each of the techniques (*Process*) listed on the *Animation Tech Tech Talk* **(Animation 5b)** list. This prepares them to be able to incorporate any of the techniques into their final animations. Oftentimes students will need to go back and add a clear demonstration of one or more of the techniques. This animation is not evaluated on neatness or for perfectly smooth transitions. The main purpose of this "practice animation" is to have students understand and demonstrate each technique before going on to a final animation production.

Note: "Bendy Guys" are plastic bendable figurines that can be purchased from novelty stores like Oriental Trading Company.

Extensions: ....

You can add a content-related concept to the Bendy Guy animation assignment. Examples include:

1. The background could be rainforest trees (science).
2. The Bendy Guy characters could demonstrate a math problem.
3. Word bubbles could be added so the characters could "recite" Shakespeare (Language Arts).

5a   Bendy Guy Plan - Technical Practice Animation

Name_____ Date _____ Total (45 points)

____ 1. I demonstrated all 10 animation techniques described on the back of this page. (10 points)

Statements of actions: What happens in each part of the animation (5 points each)?

____2. Beginning:

_____

____3. Middle:

_____

____ 4. End:

_____

____ 5. Title Page:

_____

____ 6. Credits Page:

_____

____ 7. Slide movement is reasonably smooth. I used a tripod or support to keep the pictures from being jumpy.

____ 8. Pictures are framed. There are no desk tops or other things showing (fingers, carpet, etc.).

Animation Tasks: Have each task initialed by your teacher as you complete each one.

____ a. Have a mini-conference with you teacher and get your plan approved.

____ b. Complete the Mini-Storyboard.

____ c. Take a few practice pictures and save them in a file on the computer.

____ d. Take pictures and save them in separate folders each day.

____ e. Put the pictures into the Animation Program & test it on the computer.

____ f. Get a peer to do a practice evaluation of your animation (peers initials).

____ g. Have a final mini-conference with your teacher for feedback and suggestions – edit your animation.

____ h. Present your animation to the class.

Animation Agreement: Students initial and date each of the items below.

_____ I understand the animation target due date is 2 weeks from the beginning date:

_____.

_____I understand that I may need to work outside of class to finish my project.

_____I understand that I may use any camera to take pictures.

_____I understand that I may complete the practice animation before going on to the final animation projects.

_____My partner approved by my teacher and my parent(s) is:_____

_____I am working alone on my Bendy Guy animation.

_____   _____
Student Signature   Date   Parent Signature   Date

Front Page of Plan Approved by (teacher) _____Date: _____

Points: Points are awarded during the final animation presentation.

5b

Animation Tech Talk

Complete this planning page by describing how you will demonstrate each of the following 10 techniques in your "Bendy Guy" animation. (10 points)

1. SQUASH & STRETCH	
2. ANTICIPATION	
3. FOLLOW THROUGH/ OVERLAPPING ACTION	
4. STAGING	
5. SLOW IN & SLOW OUT FAST IN & FAST OUT	
6. SECONDARY ACTIONS	
7. EXAGGERATION	
8. PATHS OF MOVEMENT	
9. CHARACTER ANALYSIS	
10. MORPHING	
11. OTHER IDEAS	

Tech Term Plan Approved by Teacher: _____ Date:

_____Points are awarded during the final animation presentation.

Bendy Guy Mini Storyboard

DETAILED ACTION STATEMENT #1	#1 BEGINNING SCENE

DETAILED ACTION STATEMENT #2	#2 MIDDLE SCENE

DETAILED ACTION STATEMENT #3	#3 ENDING SCENE

TITLE PAGE DESIGN	CREDITS PAGE DESIGN

Name _____ Animation title _____

Total pts. _____/15 (3 pts. Each section)

Animation Lesson 6: Final Animations

Objective: Students will create Final Animations to demonstrate high levels of creative thinking, technology, and animation skills.

Strategies: Animation and Technical Skills

Elements: Fluency, Flexibility, Originality, Elaboration

Fan: Person, Process, Perception, Persistence, Product, Press, Passion

CD: **6a** Final Animation Plan & Rubric
6b Final Animation Student Photos (Photo Storyboards and Animations
                              Folder) CD ONLY
6c Final Animation Storyboard

Directions: ....

This is an advanced level animation lesson involving character and background designs. Students have already been introduced to all the skills they will need to complete these projects in all of the previous lessons they have completed in the Animation Unit. They will call upon their knowledge of all of the Elements of Creativity and the skills they have developed in each area of the Creativity Fan as they design their characters and their animation plans.

1. Let students pick a media format from category A and B for their final animation productions. If time permits students can do additional formats.

   A. Coin Animation or Paper-Cut-Outs (paper characters can be made from construction paper, origami, or magazines).

   B. Chalk Animation or Clay Animation (use Plasticine™ , a non-staining and non-drying clay).

2. Remind students they will need to complete a *Final Animation Plan & Rubric* **(Animation 6a)** and a *Final Animation Storyboard* **(Animation 6c)** for each product they choose to complete. Sample student-created *Photo Storyboards and Animations* **(Animation 6b)** provide you with examples to share with students.

3. For Clay animations you will need to provide students with a material similar to Plasticine™, a non-staining and non-drying type of clay for creating their characters and objects. Larger clay characters and objects used need a form or internal structure. This can be fine wire mesh or aluminum foil. This will provide support and require less clay to complete the character or object. The internal support also assists in supporting the animation movements. You can do a Google search and get several resources including video clips to help in teaching students how to make clay figures.

4. Final animations are evaluated with the *Final Animation Rubric* **(Animation 6a)** included in this activity. Remind students that the quality of their final product is dependent upon the planning of the very minute details of character design and character movements. This would also be a good time for them to go back and review the *Animation Elaboration Log* **(Animation 4a)** they created while watching the Claymation™ videos.

Reflection: ....

Product-based activities provide teachers will many opportunities for formative assessments using mini-conferences. These give students the *"guide-on-the-side"* support they need to create rigorous creative products. It is helpful to remind students regularly that this is not about artistic talent (they can use models or clipart) to help them get started in developing their original designs. It is about the thinking and planning processes involved in the production of the animations.

Students are eager and excited to get started on the Final Animations. The development of these products will be guided by the *Final Animation Plan & Rubric* **(Animation 6a)**. At this stage most students are very independent in their work and require very little direct support from the teacher. You may schedule mini-conferences with students on an as-needed basis as they work to complete their animation.

Extensions: ....

All animations can be designed to be a complementary assignment to any core content area of instruction.

NOTES

"Creativity is inventing, experimenting, growing, taking risks, breaking rules, making mistakes, and having fun." Mary Lou Cook

6a # Final Animation Plan & Rubric

Name _____   Date _____

You must complete 2 animations:

1. ____Coin OR ____ Paper   2. ____ Clay OR ____ Chalk

Dear students: K.M.S.☺. This is your final animation project. Here is a rubric to help you get the most points for your efforts! If you finish early you can do another animation of your choice.

CHARACTER _____

SETTING/SUBJECT CONNECTION (OPTIONAL K.M.S.☺.) _____

PLOT/MAIN IDEA _____

FEELING/EMOTION _____

ANIMATION TECHNIQUES (3): _____

TASK	0-2 Points	3-5 Points	6-8 Points	9-10 Points	**Points**
100 PICTURES	0-49	50-69	70-89	90-100	
BACKGROUND EFFECT	LITTLE	SOME	A LOT	K.M.S.☺.	
CHARACTER DESIGN	MINIMAL	OK	GOOD	K.M.S.☺.	
ELABORATION/ MOVEMENT	NONE	SOME	MANY	INCREDIBLE	
CREATIVITY PLOT	BORING	OK	INTER-ESTING	K.M.S.☺.	
NEATNESS	MESSY	UNTIDY	TIDY	PRECISE	
SLIDE MOVEMENT	VERY ER-RATIC	LITTLE JUMPY	MOSTLY SMOOTH	VERY SMOOTH	
TECHNIQUES USED	0	1	2	3	
CROPPED PICTURES	FEW	SOME	MOST	ALL	
PATHS OF MOVEMENT	0	1	2	3	
Ready to Present	4th Day	3rd Day	2nd Day	1st Day	
				Total Points	

100 Pictures = minimum requirement. If the animation has less the grade will start at that percent, e.g. 79 pictures = 79%. Any points deducted from the rubric will then be deducted from 79.

PROJECT CALENDAR OF DUE DATES	DATE ASSIGNED	DATE DUE	DATE IN
1. I was given this Individual Animation Assignment			
2. I explained the project (signed) to my parent(s) on			
3. My 3Paragraph Creative Animation Story is due on			
4. My storyboard is due on			
5. My 100 pictures are due on			
6. My animation is due on my teacher's computer file			
7. I will be ready to present on			

MAIN CHARACTER(S) DESIGNS	OBJECT(S) DESIGNS

Students: please read and initial each statement below:

1. _____ I explained this assignment and my subject connection (optional) to my parents.

2. _____ I showed my parents my assignment dates I ENTERED on my monthly calendar.

3. _____ I understand that I may need to work outside of class to finish this project.

_____ _____   _____
Date   Student   Parent

Students: Now you know all the techniques and skills! Practice your presentation so you can . . . K.M.S.☺!

6c

Final Animation Storyboard

Students you are required to list 5 or more details actions for each scene.

5 DETAILED ACTION STATEMENTS #1	DRAW OR SKETCH A DETAILED BEGINNING SCENE #1

5 DETAILED ACTION STATEMENTS #2	DRAW OR SKETCH A DETAILED MIDDLE SCENE #2

5 DETAILED ACTION STATEMENTS #3	DRAW OR SKETCH DETAILED ENDING SCENES #3

FINAL ANIMATION STORY-BOARD TITLE PAGE DESIGN	CREDITS PAGE DESIGN

Name _____

Animation title _____

Total pts. _____/40 (10 pts. Each page)

IX Brain Unit

Overview: Students will work in a long-term unit to build skills for 21st Century Learning. These skills include: creative thinking, critical thinking, problem solving, collaboration, and communication.

Curriculum Standards Connections:

The unit has a strong science content connection with activities and extensions that apply to many content areas.

Elements: Fluency, Flexibility, Originality, and Elaboration

Fan: Person, Persistence, Process, Product, Press, Perception, and Passion

Directions: ....

This is a multi-stage, product-based learning unit that works well in a creative thinking enrichment class or in a science classroom. The Famous Character Brains lessons can be used as an introductory or culminating activity in various content areas. The following is an outline of the curricular design for this unit:

Brain 1: Brain Roadmap Lesson
    1a Brain Facts & Functions "That's Me"
    1b Brain Roadmap Handout
    1c Brain Roadmap Memory Sentences – Student Samples
    1d Brain Roadmap Test
Brain 2: Pathway of Thought Lesson
    2a Teacher Neuron Diagram
    2b Student Neuron Diagram
    2c Dendrite Growth Patterns
    2d Brain Cell Test
    2e Brain Anatomy & Physiology Learning Test
Brain 3: Brain Show and Tell Lesson
    3a Brain Show and Tell Tic-Tac-Toe
Brain 4: Famous Character Brains Lesson
    4a Famous Character Brain Think Tank
    4b Right Brain Handout
    4c Left Brain Handout
    4d Student Sample – Einstein's Brain
    4e Famous Character Brain Writing

Brain Lesson 1: **Brain Roadmaps**

Objective: 1. Students will pre-assess their knowledge and understanding of their brains.

2. Students will identify the "thinking sections" of their brains.

Strategies: That's Me, Anchoring

Elements: Fluency, Flexibility, Originality

Fan: Product, Perception

CD: **1a** Brain Facts & Function "That's Me"
1b Brain Roadmap Handout
1c Brain Roadmap Memory Sentences – Student Samples CD ONLY
1d Brain Roadmap Test

Directions: ....

1. Complete a "That's Me" using the *Brain Facts & Function* handout **(Brain 1a)**. As you read the statements, tell students you are going to share with them information about brains that is True or False. Tell them to stand up and say "That's me!" if they believe (*Perception*) the statement you read is true. Read a statement from the "That's Me" Brain Facts & Functions list. After you complete the "That's Me" activity with the students, give them a copy of the handout so they can understand and remember the brain facts and functions for their upcoming *Brain Roadmap Test* **(Brain 1d).**

2. Give students the *Brain Roadmap* Handout **(Brain 1b)** with the functions of the thinking sections of the brain labeled. Briefly discuss each area's function in a question and answer session. It is fun to include in the discussion with students the fact that their pre-frontal lobe (decision making area) has latent development. Additionally, recall the phrase "Eyes in the back of your head" and ask if they see a connection with the map (occipital lobe at the very back).

3. Have students pair with a partner to write one or two memory sentences to help them remember the order of the areas (Fluency and Flexibility). Give students time to create the memory sentences (Originality). Each word of the sentence will begin with the letter of the alphabet for the beginning letter of the <u>FUNCTIONS</u> (sequentially) for each area of the brain. These memory sentences will trigger student recall of the order of the FUNCTIONS of the areas of the brain. If they finish early, have students study the map as an Anchoring activity to prepare for the test they will be having on the FUNCTIONS of the areas of the brain. Tell students the scientific names of the areas will be optional on the test.

4. Bring the class back to the front of the room and share B*rain Roadmap Memory Sentences* **(Brain 1c)** on a White Board, Blog, Google doc, etc.

5. Test students over the sections of the brain in the near future.

Reflection: ....

The "That's Me" activity is a fun and engaging way to pre-assess student knowledge or level of understanding for any unit of study. It can also be used formatively and summatively to assess student learning. The brain "That's Me" questions have been constructed to be intentionally ambiguous and/or provoking to stimulate the discussion of opinions and beliefs (*Perception*) regarding this topic. When students have an emotional response to being right or wrong, it further etches those understanding on their brains. This thinking anatomy lesson is very interesting to most students and they enjoy the fun memory sentences. When the memory sentences (*Product*) are shared, some students elect to use ones created by other students instead of their own to help them prepare for the test.

Extension: ....

1. Ask student teams to formulate interesting, fun, and original questions they would like to ask the class on a particular topic of study to create a "That's Me" activity. You can also ask students to find more questions they would like to add to the Brain "That's Me" and then pose them at the beginning of class as a Brain Starter activity.

2. Memory sentences are creative and effective ways to learn some basic information. Most of us remember using it to learn the order of the planets. "Many very early maps just show us nine planets" was a phrase used in school to trigger the memory of the names of the planets.

BRAIN ROADMAP TEST ANSWER KEY

1. PROBLEM SOLVING	FRONTAL LOBE
2. MOVING	MOTOR CORTEX
3. FEELING	SENSORY CORTEX
4. TOUCHING	PARIETAL LOBE
5. SEEING	OCCIPITAL LOBE
6. BALANCING	CEREBELUM
7. PATHWAY TO BODY	BRAIN STEM
8. AROUSAL	RETICULAR FORMATION
9. READING	WERNICKE'S AREA
10. HEARING	TEMPORAL LOBE
11. SPEECH	BROCA'S AREA

Note: Use the "That's Me" to grade the optional question on the test.

ALL THE EVEN NUMBERS ON "THAT'S ME" ARE FALSE.

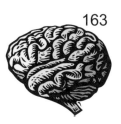

1a Brain Facts & Function "That's Me"

____ 1. The brain weighs about as much as a bag of sugar.

____ 2. The number of dendrites in our brains does not change.

____ 3. Human brains are getting bigger.

____ 4. The brain rests while we are sleeping.

____ 5. Use it or lose it" applies to our brains.

____ 6. Your brain power is inherited.

____ 7. The brain is 80% water.

____ 8. Reasoning will most usually rule over your emotions.

____ 9. Male & female brains function quite differently.

____ 10. Alcohol actually stimulates the brain.

____ 11. The brain does not work like a computer.

____ 12. You can stop thinking on command.

____ 13. Einstein's brain was larger than most brains.

____ 14. The brain cannot receive messages from your senses.

____ 15. There enough electricity in the brain to turn on a light bulb.

____ 16. The brain messages travel in your body faster than an Indy race car.

____ 17. Boys lose brain cells faster than girls.

____ 18. Girls' brains are bigger than boys' brains.

____ 19. The brain has filters to keep out information.

____ 20. The brain holds as much information as two encyclopedias.

(Adapted from Brain Compatible Classrooms by Robin Fogarty, 1997)

1b   **Brain Roadmap Handout**

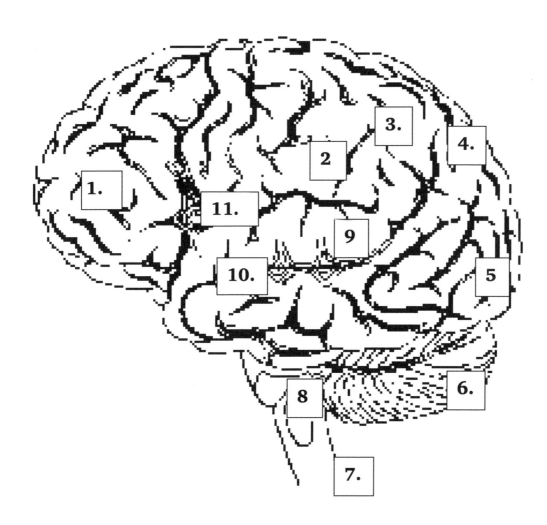

1. FRONTAL LOBE = PROBLEM SOLVING

2. MOTOR CORTEX = MOVING

3. SENSORY CORTEX = FEELING

4. PARIETAL LOBE = TOUCHING

5. OCCIPITAL LOBE = SEEING

6. CEREBELLUM = BALANCING

7. BRAIN STEM = PATHWAY TO BODY

8. RETICULAR FORMATION = AROUSAL/AWARENESS

9. WERNICKE'S AREA = READING

10. TEMPORAL LOBE = HEARING

11. BROCA'S AREA = SPEECH

1d

Brain Roadmap Test

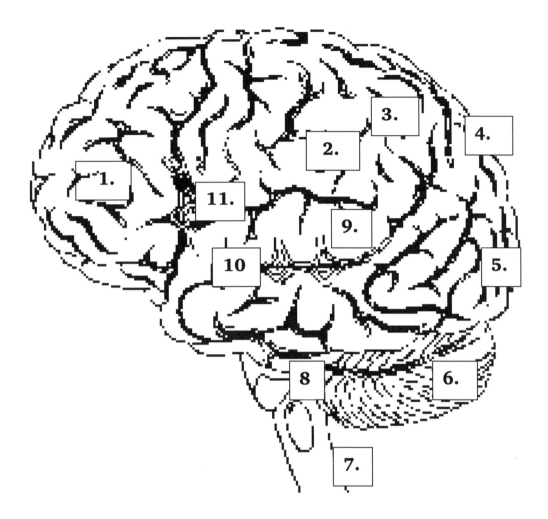

Write the function or process for each section of the brain labeled above.

List the scientific names of each area for extra credit (optional).

1._____   2. _____

3. _____   4. _____

5. _____   6. _____

7. _____   8. _____

9. _____   10. _____

                                                     11. _____

Optional K.M.S.☺. (5pts): Discuss, debate, or explain five of the brain Fact and Function "That's Me" statements.

Brain Lesson 2: **Pathway of Thought**

Objective: Students will understand how thought travels in the brain and in the body.

Strategies: Direct Instruction, Simulation

Elements: Elaboration and Originality

Fan: Perception

CD: **2a** Teacher Neuron Diagram
                   2b Student Neuron Diagram
                   2c Dendrite Growth Patterns
                   2d Brain Cell Test
                   2e Brain Anatomy & Physiology Learning Test

Directions (Part I): Brain Cell Anatomy and Pathway of Thought.................

Distribute the *Student Neuron* handout **(Brain 2b)** to students. Give them a mini-lecture (Direct Instruction) on the anatomy of the neuron and how the pathway thought travels in their brains. Have students take notes on the diagram to understand the anatomy and the pathway of thought. They will need this information for their test.

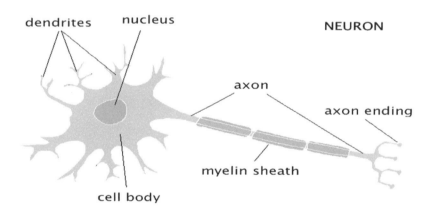

Mini-lecture Facts **(Brain 2a)** *Teacher Neuron* handout):

Neurons are the nerve cells inside the brain. Here is information you can share in your lecture. If you like, you can find more facts on the Internet depending on the age of your students.

1. Cell body – central round part of the neuron cell.
2. Axon - long fiber of the neuron that sends electrical impulses 100 mph.
3. Dendrites – short branches that receive chemical impulses.
4. Neural Network – group of connected neurons.
5. Synapse – space between neurons in the brain where the messages are chemical.
6. Myelin Sheath – fatty covering of axons that allows impulses (messages) to move faster.
7. Electrochemical Reaction - the messages are chemical between the dendrites (in the synapse) and electrical as they travel along the axon.

8. Body Messages – neurons receive messages from the senses, muscles, or other neurons at a rate of approximately 100 mph.

9. Brain Messages - travel 250 mph in the brain (faster than an Indianapolis 500 race car).

Directions (Part II): Neuron Simulations ....

1. Have student partners use their arms to simulate the pathway of thought between two neurons. The *Teacher Neuron* diagram **(Brain 2a)** provides labeled neuron parts with associated student body parts. The students' arms become the "talking neurons" to explain the parts and functions as part of the simulation. Encourage students to use humor (exaggeration and puns) as they perform their simulation.

2. Discuss the phrase "use it or lose it" as it applies to the brain. Show students the diagram *Dendrite Growth Patterns* **(Brain 2c)** - maps of the neuron paths of a newborn, three- month old, 15-month old, and finally a two-year old. Have students journal for three to five minutes their reaction or explanation of the changes they observe in the diagram. Here is a set of sample prompts for the journaling and follow-up discussion *(Perception)*:

1. Ask students to reflect on what they see.
2. What do they think causes the changes in the brain maps?
3. Do they believe they can affect the design of their own "brain maps?" How?
4. Do they believe if they coast in school for a length of time, they can "catch up" with their brain map design later?
3. Give Students the *Brain Cell Test* **(Brain 2d).**

Directions (Part III): Neuron Patterns ....

Show students some of the beautiful laser-enhanced photographs of neurons (Google some examples). Assign them the task of creating their own artistic version of neurons. Have them color-code a legend to identify the parts, the pathway of thought, and the types of transmission occurring in the different sections. Remind students they will have a test on the anatomy and pathway of thought.

Reflection: ....

Students find it rather interesting to discover the pathway of thought and enjoy the partner anatomy pathway practice of recreating the path of thought with a partner. The Neuron Chain of Thought creatively engages students in the anatomy lesson with connections to your language arts curriculum.

Extension: ....

1. **Neuron Chain of Thought**

End class with a "Neuron Chain of Thought." Select a student to start a creative story *(Originality)* by standing up in the neuron pose (arms spread apart). This student starts with a creative story line and then calls out another student's name to join *(Elaboration)* the neuron chain. This student assumes the neuron position near the other student (keeping a synapse space) and adds a story line. Continue until all students have joined the thought chain. Remind students to remember their segment of the story line. When all have joined, start back at the beginning and quickly re-tell the complete story.

2. **Brain Anatomy and Physiology Learning Test**

Give students the *Brain Anatomy and Physiology Learning Test* **(Brain 2e).** Then provide some form of direct instruction or a fact finding activity to teach students the basic anatomy and physiology of the brain. One version is to give the students the test and let them fill in the blanks as a mini-web research activity. Students could also add other facts to the test from their research. Another version is to lecture to the students and have them create a draft of a mind map as they take notes. If you wish, the Brain Anatomy and Physiology Learning Test can be administered as a test after the learning occurs.

Brain Anatomy & Physiology Learning Test

Answer Key

K__ 1.	H__ 9.	Y__ 17.	24 – 25
L__ 2.	T__ 10.	D__ 18.	electrochemical
O__ 3.	F__ 11.	N__ 19.	F__ 26.
E__ 4.	G__ 12.	S__ 20.	M__ 27.
B__ 5	W__ 13.	M__ 21.	F__28.
P__ 6.	N__ 14.	Y__ 22.	M__ 29.
I__ 7.	A__ 15.	A___ 23.	F___30.
R__ 8.	Q__ 16.		M__ 31.

32-35

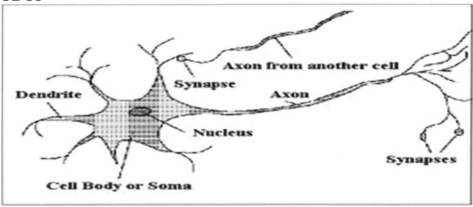

36 – 40

In your own words, describe how messages are received and sent in the brain. (4 or more thoughts)
Sample answers 36-40:
1. The neurons receive messages from the senses, muscles, or other neurons.
2. The messages are processed in the cell (neuron) and sent out to other neurons by traveling on the axon.
3. When the messages get to the end of the axon near the dendrite branches they become chemical and travel across the synapse space.
4. Messages in the brain travel 250 mph and in the body travel 100 mph.

2a

Teacher Neuron Diagram

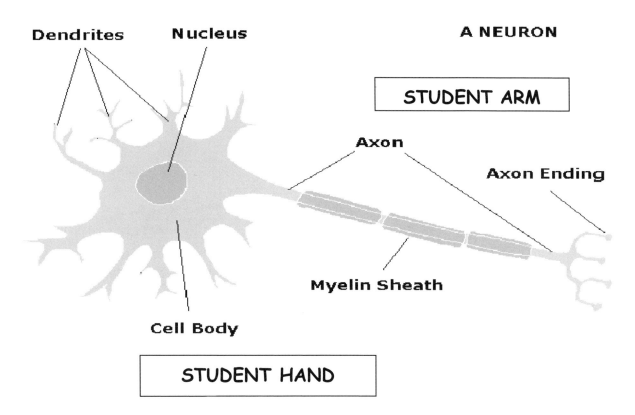

STUDENT FINGERS

Dendrites   Nucleus   A NEURON

STUDENT ARM

Axon

Axon Ending

Myelin Sheath

Cell Body

STUDENT HAND

Note: The student labels represent the body parts students will use in re-creating the pathway of thought as a simulation with a partner.

2b

Student Neuron Diagram

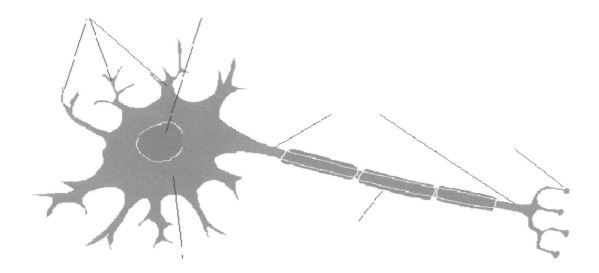

2c

Dendrite Growth Patterns

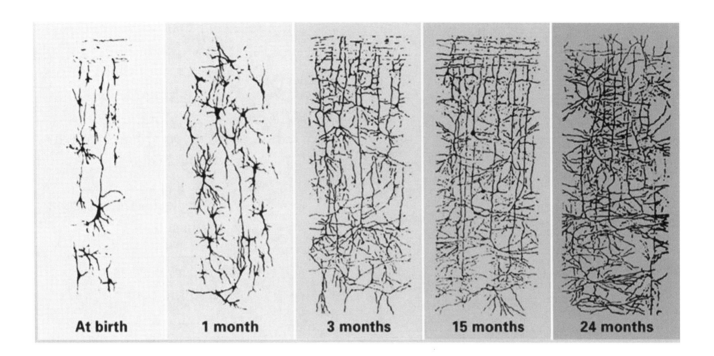

| At birth | 1 month | 3 months | 15 months | 24 months |

2d

Brain Cell Test

Name _____   Date _____

1. Draw and label the brain cell below:
   dendrites, nucleus, axons, cell body, and myelin sheath.

Directions: Answer the following questions.

1. How fast does thought travel in the brain?
   _____

2. What type of message travels in the brain?
   _____

3. What picks up the message in the brain?
   _____

4. What part carries the message to the body?
   _____

5. How fast does the message go to the body?
   _____

6. What type of message goes to the body?
   _____

7. What three things can brain cells get messages from?
   a. _____
   b. _____
   c. _____

8. What kind of reaction describes the message transfer process in both the brain and the body?

   _____

   _____

2e
Brain Anatomy & Physiology Learning Test

Name _____ Date _____

Matching: select the answer from the list.

_____ 1. We have _____ nerve cells in the brain.

_____ 2. Messages travel _____ in the brain.

_____ 3. The brain weighs _____ of your body weight.

_____ 4. The brain uses _____ of the energy in the body.

_____ 5. The study of the brain is _____.

_____ 6. The study of the mind is _____.

_____ 7. The brain generates _____ of electricity.

_____ 8. The average brain weighs _____.

_____ 9. The brain is about the size of half a(n)_____.

_____ 10. Several billion bits of information pass through the brain (time).

_____ 11. The brain is protected by the _____.

_____ 12. The brain feels like a ripe _____.

_____ 13. The surface of the brain looks like a _____.

_____ 14. The brain cells that make up the brain are called _____.

_____ 15. The path the impulses (messages) travel on is the _____.

_____ 16. The messages travel on the path (how fast) _____.

_____ 17. The space between the brain cells is called the _____.

_____ 18. The _____ receive the impulses.

The neurons receive and send messages from: _____

19. _____ 20. _____21. _____

22. Messages are chemical in the brain in the _____.

23. Messages are electrical in the brain in the _____.

Fill in the blank (2 words).

The way messages are sent and received in the brain is called a(n)

24 - 25_____   _____.

Label the characteristics of the brain. F = Female M = Male

_____ 26. Express emotions easily

_____ 27. Lose brain cells 3 times as fast

_____ 28. Learn to read earlier

_____ 29. 15% larger brain

_____ 30. Rely on memory to find places, not maps

_____ 31. Express themselves through gestures

ANSWERS: SOME MAY BE USED MORE THAN ONCE. SOME ARE NOT USED.

A. AXONS	H. CANTALOUPE	N. NEURO 2 %	U. PEACH
B. BIOLOGY	I. 25 WATTS	O. PSYCHOLOGY	V. WALNUT
C. CHEMICAL	J. 50 WATTS	P. 100 MPH	W. 5 POUNDS
D. DENDRITES	K. 100	Q. 3 POUNDS	X. SYNAPSE
E. 20%	BILLION	R. SENSES	Y. ELECTRICAL
F. CRANIUM	L. 250 MPH	S. EVERY SECOND	
G. AVOCADO	M. MUSCLES	T. EVERY MINUTE	

32 – 35. Draw and Label the neuron.

36 – 40. In your own words, describe how messages are received and sent in the brain. (4 or more thoughts)

Brain Lesson 3: Brain Show and Tell

Objectives: 1. To demonstrate knowledge of the anatomy, physiology, or the learning characteristics of the brain through the development of a creative product.

Strategies: Independent Study, Presentation Skills

Elements: Fluency, Flexibility, Originality, Elaboration

Fan: Product, Person, Passion, Process, Perception, Persistence

CD: **3a** Brain Show and Tell Tic-Tac-Toe

Directions: ....

The student will select three products from the *Brain Show and Tell Tic-Tac-Toe* **(Brain 3a)** to complete during this unit of study. All students are required to do the center block *Famous Character Brains.*

Reflection: ....

This lesson is a fun and engaging way to assess student knowledge or level of understanding. This assignment can be given to students early in the unit of study so you can intersperse product work days throughout the unit. You can also schedule three or more presentation days for students to present their work to the class. See the Passion Learning Unit for sample product calendars and a rubric you can use for evaluating the products.

Extensions: ....

Students can present their final products as mini-teaching sessions. This could be done in a rotation format of learning centers in the classroom or as more formal presentations for the whole class.

NOTES

> **"It is good to rub and polish our brain against that of other."**
> **Montainge**

Brain Show & Tell
Tic-Tac-Toe

3a

#1 WRITE & PERFORM A RIGHT & LEFT BRAIN COMEDY SKIT	**#2** PHOTO ESSAY BRAIN FACTS USING A WEB 2.0 TOOL	**#3** BRAIN WEB WIKI WITH PODCASTS
#4 ABC CHILDREN'S BRAIN ANATOMY BOOK	**#5** FAMOUS CHARACTER BRAINS	**#6** FAMOUS BRILLIANT BRAINS GLOSTERS/ POSTERS
#7 PARODY A BRAIN SONG	**#8** OTHER: SEE TEACHER	**#9** CREATE A BRAIN GENDER BOARD GAME

ALL PRODUCTS MUST HAVE 15 OR MORE FASCINATING FACTS.

I have selected items: #__5___,   #_____ & #_____

_____   _____
Student Signature   Date   Parent Signature   Date

Brain Lesson 4: Famous Character "Brains"

Objectives: 1. Students will learn about famous individuals' characteristics and world contributions.

2. Students will use creativity and humor to understand and portray the "brains" of famous people.

Strategies: Brain Writing, Brain Walk, Piggyback, Brainstorm

Elements: Fluency, Flexibility, Originality, and Elaboration

Fan: Perception, Product

CD: **4a** Famous Character Brain Think Tank
4b Right Brain Template CD ONLY
4c Left Brain Template CD ONLY
4d Einstein Brain - Student Sample CD ONLY
4e Famous Character Brain Writing Handout

Directions: ....

1. Decide whose brain you want students to examine and/or let them brainstorm a list of ideas related to an instructional goal. The choices could be content-related or from historical figures, occupations, literary characters, doctors, book characters, rock stars, sports stars, or actors/actresses, etc.

2. Use the *Famous Character Brain Think Tank* **(Brain 4a)** to generate attributes or characteristics of their person. Encourage students to use humor and exaggeration. As an example, consider the brain of a *doctor*. What are some of the physical, verbal, visual, social, and mental attributes or characteristics that come to mind? How about:

- Physical: Listening to your heart, operating
- Verbal: "Take two aspirin and call me in the morning."
- Visual: White coat and stethoscope
- Social: Playing golf
- Mental: Diagnosing your symptoms

3. Another Brainstorming technique you may want to have students try is an activity called Brain Writing. This method of brainstorming allows students to generate ideas (Fluency) anonymously. They can hitch onto the ideas of others by focusing on the Piggyback rule of brainstorming.

4. Have students use the *Famous Character Brain Writing* Handout **(4e)**. Each person in the group needs one sheet (this works best with three or five students per group). As students think of ideas, they write them down in one of the spaces provided. Next they put their sheet in the middle of the table and take a sheet left there by another student. Continue this process for five-to-ten minutes, or until all sheets are filled. Next, students can complete a Brain Walk from table to table on the teacher's command to continue the Brain Writing process on other groups' sheets.

5. Once the above lists have been generated through Brain Writing, students can decide for each statement whether it fits better in the right brain or the left brain (see Right and Left Activities in Climate Section). At this point it is also fun to determine proportions. For example, it may be funny to have a large area for *golf* and a very small area for *patience (Perception)*. Remind students to use *exaggeration* as it is an incredibly effective technique that combines creativity and humor.

6. Now use the empty *Right and Left Brain Templates* **(Brain 4b, 4c)** to put all ideas into either the right or left side (*Product*).

Reflection: ....

This activity was originally developed to poke fun at (satire) recent brain research involving brain hemisphericity. This is a fun and interesting product that can be designed to meet many curricular or content-based goals. Show the sample student product of *Einstein's Brain* **(Brain 4d).** This activity has been included as a requirement on the Brain Show and Tell Tic-Tac-Toe in this unit.

Extensions: ....

For individual or group work (to be shared with the entire class):

1. ART: draw pictures inside the brain instead of using words.

2. SCIENCE: create the brain of an animal or plant.

3. GEOGRAPHY: create the brain of an inanimate object such as the Statue of Liberty, the Washington Monument, or Devil's Tower.

4. CAREERS: use this activity as an individual or class assignment as you explore various occupations.

5. HISTORY: use historical facts from your text (or other sources) as well as stories and myths associated with the person and compare and contrast the brains of two presidents.

6. PSYCHOLOGY: tie this in with a study of personality profiles.

7. ANATOMY: take various parts of the brain (cerebrum, cerebral cortex, corpus callosum, etc.) and generate right or left brain statements about the function of each.

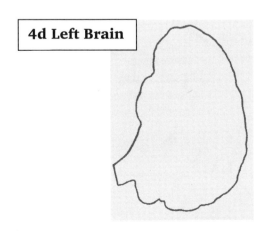

4d Left Brain

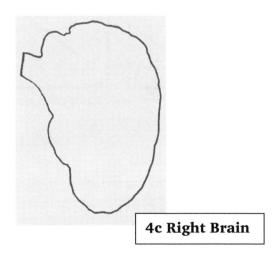

4c Right Brain

Famous Character Brain Think Tank

4a

	PHYSICAL	VERBAL	VISUAL	SOCIAL	MENTAL
1					
2					
3					
4					
5					

NAME_____   DATE_____

4e
Famous Character Brain Writing

Famous Person:	
SAYINGS	APPEARANCE
LIKES & DISLIKES	ACTIONS

X Passion Learning Unit

Overview:	Students will work in a long-term unit to build skills for 21st Century Learning. These skills include: creative thinking, critical thinking, problem solving, collaboration, and communication.
Elements:	Fluency, Flexibility, Originality, Elaboration
Fan:	Person, Persistence, Process, Product, Press, Perception, and Passion

Summary: ....

We all agree that today's students need to be prepared for tomorrow's world. The 21st century initiatives now encourage educators to teach using creativity as part of their instructional processes. Creativity involves both the development of *creative thinking* and *critical thinking* skills. These are recognized as part of the skill sets that will make students useful and productive contributors to society. The development of these skills, along with the associated attitudes needed to make this successful, require student learning that involves sustained efforts over a long period of time. This is one of the basic premises of teaching with *creativity* - the honing and refining of both products and skills over a long period of time.

One of the major difficulties for teachers is the detailed planning of long-term product-based units. The Passion Learning Unit provides templates, timelines, and a basic planning and organization structure that can be modified to fit a variety of product-based learning environments. This unit could be used to study any topic of interest or famous individual.

The presentations of the products are scheduled over a generous period of time. Some students, of course, will finish much faster than others. Remind students that in a learning classroom it is OK to finish quickly, but it is not OK to stop learning. So the choices they have are 1) to continue, with your consultation and the consultation of their peers, 2) to improve one or more products or 3) to start a new product. Starting an additional product or working on the ones they have already developed oftentimes results in K.M.S.☺. student outcomes!

This is a multi-stage product-based learning unit designed to be integrated into a regular teaching curriculum or taught as a stand-alone enrichment course. The following curricular design for the Passion Learning Unit is meant to be used sequentially as a means to integrate creative learning opportunities into any content area. This unit includes templates and planning resources to assist you in implementing Passion Learning units of study.

Handouts:

Passion Learning 1:	Journal Essay Prompts
Passion Learning 2:	Student Introduction Letter
Passion Learning 3:	DVD Passion Log
	a. Passion Log - Student Sample CD ONLY
Passion Learning 4:	Topic Alpha Think Tank
	a. Passion Learning Topic List
Passion Learning 5:	Famous People Think Tank

Passion Learning 6:   Student Organization & Planning Calendar
                                              a. Tic-Tac-Toe
Passion Learning 7:   Important Questions
Passion Learning 8:   Presentation Rubric & Fact Sheet
Passion Learning 9:   Blank Tic-Tac-Toe CD only
Passion Learning 10:   Teacher Planning & Organization Calendar

Teachers: ....

1. You will select a video of a famous, passionate person(s) to show students over a period of several weeks for inspiration and demonstration of passionate pursuits. They will complete the Passion Learning Video Log while viewing the video. I showed my middle school students: *Shackleton - The Greatest Survival Story of All Time* (2002).

2. The products the students create are not about the individual. The products are about things the individual might produce or about their accomplishments. Each product must contain 15 pieces of research information. Examples:

   1. A newspaper article written by Thomas Edison about one of his inventions.

   2. An Orville and Wilbur Wright podcast journal about their attempted flights.

> *"Creativity is a central source of meaning in our lives . . . when we are involved in it, we feel that we are living more fully than during the rest of life." Mihaly Csikszentmihalyi*

1 JOURNAL ESSAY PROMPTS

Students: please focus on the Element of Elaboration (Details! Details! Details!) as you begin your writing. Support your comments and answers by explaining (more details!) your statements/beliefs.

First Paragraph:

1. What is passion learning?
2. How is it different from other types of learning?
3. How are interests, hobbies, and passions different from each other?

Second Paragraph:

1. Which adult(s) do you know, or have heard of, who have passion areas of learning (including teachers, family members, or famous people)?
2. How do they demonstrate they have a passion area of learning?
3. How do you think this affects their life?

Third Paragraph

1. Can subjects in school be passion areas of learning?
2. What changes would you make to classrooms to make them passion learning classrooms?
3. How do you think passion learning could change your life?

NOTE: Teachers are encouraged to give these questions to students over several days (as journal prompts) to get more focused and intense work from them. After students have responded in journal format, you can then assign them to write a final essay using their responses.

2   Student Introduction Letter

Dear Students:

You are about to conduct an in-depth Passion Learning (PL) investigation to explore a topic or person you want to learn more about. Each of you will be given a product choice board (Tic-Tac-Toe) to choose the products you will use to demonstrate your learning and creativity. This board has been designed with you in mind, and offers you a variety of ways to demonstrate your new knowledge and skills. You will begin by spending time gathering ideas and resources to help you choose your area of study. Look at your learning style preferences and the creative product list to choose products that you really like to do. Here's your opportunity to direct your own learning, so pick carefully - make sure your topic is worthy of your best effort. So let's begin!

Here is your "TO DO" List:

Passion Learning Alpha Think Tank: Complete a Passion Learning Alpha Think Tank to begin getting ideas for an area of study. You may use any available resources to help you create the Alpha Think Tank.

Passion Learning Person Think Tank: Next you will complete a Passion Learning Think Tank on five people you find the most interesting. Start investigating the person with website resources and books from the library. Once you have your Think Tank completed, have a mini-conference with your teacher to make the final decision to select the person you will study and to choose your products.

Passion Learning Tic-Tac-Toe: You will complete three squares (products) and present them to the class. If you finish early you may choose to do more in-depth work on one of your products or start an additional product.

Presentation Partner: Pick a presentation partner to assist you during your presentation. You can help each other in a variety of ways: holding projects, asking interview questions, introducing your comedy routine, etc. (Optional)

Passion Learning Planning & Organization Calendar: Review this with your teacher during your conference and ask any questions you may have at this time. You will get signatures from your teacher as you complete each preparation requirement.

Students: review this letter with your parents and return the signed letter to me.

_____   _____

    Parent Signature (date)   Student Signature (date)

    Sincerely,

3	DVD PASSION LOG	
INTERESTS	**HOBBIES**	**PASSIONS**

PASSION LEARNING (YOUR PERSON)
INVESTIGATION LOG

INTERESTS	**HOBBIES**	**PASSIONS**

DIRECTIONS: Students: Watch the famous person DVD and record the interests, hobbies, and passions you see the main character portray. Additionally, as you research your passion person, make a note of their interests, hobbies, and passions on the lower half of this page. The goal for this assignment is to record five or more items in each category.

4

Topic Alpha Think Tank

A	B	C	D	E
F	G	H	i	J
K	L	M	N	O
P	Q	R	S	T
U	V	W	Y	Z

Students: Look up the definition for any Passion Learning Topics you don't know. Write the definition on the back of the page.

4a Passion Learning Topic List

acrobat	convict	innkeeper	painter	surfer
actor	cook	introvert	parson	swindler
airman	counterfeiter	inventor	patron	swordsman
amateur	coward	jailor	philanthropist	tattler
ambassador	cowboy	janitor	philosopher	teenager
anchorman	crook	jazzman	photographer	terrorist
angler	dancer	joker	physician	tyrant
animal keeper	dandy	journalist	pilgrim	umpire
animator	deranged	judge	pirate	uncle
artist	detective	judo master	planter	unhealthy
astrologer	dictator	jury	poet	vagabond
athlete	director	king	policeman	vandal
attorney	diver	knight	preacher	vanquished
author	doctor	landlord	primate	vaudevillian
bad mouther	dreamer	lawyer	primitive	vendor
bachelor	duke	lazy person	prince/princess	victim
back woodser	chauffeur	librarian	prisoner	villain
balloonist	chef	lobbyist	psychiatrist	violinist
bandit	chemist	lumberjack	quack	waif
bandmaster	clerk	madman	repairman	waiter
banker	comedian	maid	revolutionary	warbler
barber	composer	malcontent	robber	washerwoman
beau	computer geek	manic	sailor	watchman
beggar	eavesdropper	marshal	salesman	wit
belle	elderly	mayor	scholar	wrangler
blowhard	entrepreneur	millionaire	schoolmaster	wrestler
boatswain	evangelist	minstrel	scientist	xenophobe
bodyguard	experimenter	miser	scout	x-ray
bookkeeper	fanatic	mortician	seaman	xtra
bookworm	farmer	motorcyclist	shepherd	Yankee
botanist	father	mountaineer	shopkeeper	yes-man
braggart	ferryman	navigator	sightseer	zoologist
brain	fisherman	nerd	singer	
bridegroom	forger	nurse	skipper	
bridesmaid	frogman	oracle	skydiver	
burglar	gardener	other:	smoker	
butcher	general		social worker	
cannoneer	genius		spaceman	
cartoonist	grocer		speaker	
cavalryman	guard		spendthrift	
caveman	hacker		spinster	
chairman	homeless		spy	
congressman	humorist		stevedore	
con-man	indigent		street cleaner	
connoisseur	infidel		stuntman	

Adapted from an original list by Phil Eastman, United Productions of America (UPA), (1948).

Directions:

Students will work with a partner to create an Alpha Think Tank of areas of study using words from this list matching the letter of the alphabet.

1. After selecting the word, they must research and add the name of an individual to each box. This must be an individual who has made a major contribution to our world. This change could be viewed as either positive or negative.

2. Each partner will then select five possible "candidates" to study for their Passion Learning Projects. Partners may not select the same individuals.

3. Each partner will put the names of the individuals they have selected on the Famous People Think Tank handout and find five fascinating facts for each person.

4. Partners then meet in a min-conference with their teacher to make the final selection of the person they will use for their investigation. During this time students will receive the following handouts:

    A. Planning & Organization Calendar

    B. Product Alpha Think Tank

    C. Tic-Tac-Toe (product choice board)

6. Students will not be able to study the same individual. Choices will be made on a "first-come first-served" basis and be posted in the classroom.

> *"A creative person is someone who is not afraid to try new ideas. They can go wild and crazy without feeling bad. They let in new ideas and try them. Creative people can put ideas together well and they're able to share them. They like to "make a statement" about things."*
> *~ Shilo, 7th grade student*

5   Famous People Think Tank

PERSON					
EDUCATION					
FAMILY					
I BET YOU DIDN'T KNOW THIS					
SUCCESSES					
FAILURES					

Name _____ Date _____

Directions: Students: Complete this Think Tank by researching five individuals who have made famous contributions to our world. These individuals must have made their contributions over 100 years ago. If you find someone more recent you would like to study, you must see your teacher for approval. Your teacher will decide if the individual's contributions have changed the world. Put the names of five individuals at the top of the columns. You will provide "fascinating facts" in each row that match the listed category of information. You may use the back of this sheet if you need more space.

6   Student Organization & Planning Calendar

Name _____   Date _____

ITEM	QUESTIONS TO ASK YOURSELF	POINTS & INTIALS
JOURNAL ESSAY	• Does your essay have 3 paragraphs? • Does each paragraph have 5 or more thoughts? • Did you have another student read, comment, and initial your essay before turning it in? • Did you make changes after your peer consultation?	
ALPHA THINK TANK PASSION TOPICS	• Did you circle 25 interest words on the PL Topic List before you started the Topic Alpha Think Tank? • Did you look up unknown words & write the definitions on the back of the Topic Alpha Think Tank?	
FAMOUS PEOPLE THINK TANK	• Did you select 5 different people than your partner? • Did you complete and follow all directions for the Think Tank? • Did you find fascinating facts that are not boring to you?	
FIVE IMPORTANT QUESTIONS	• Are your questions big and important enough to find out about? • Did you make sure your questions do not ask for opinions and that they are fact-finding questions?	
TEACHER MINI PASSION PERSON CONFERENCE	• Can you explain why you chose your Passion Learning Person to your teacher? • Do you have some ideas for the products you want to produce?	
25 FACTS & DATA CARDS	• Did you gather interesting and important facts? • Have you checked with another classmate to see which facts they think are the most interesting?	

ITEM	QUESTIONS TO ASK YOURSELF	POINTS & INTIALS
OTHER IDEAS/ QUESTIONS YOU HAVE TO TALK TO YOUR TEACHER ABOUT ITEM	QUESTIONS TO ASK YOURSELF	
TIC- TAC- TOE	• Did you visit at least 5 sites? • Did you find at least 3 pieces of information from 5 different sites? • Did you complete the Tic-Tac-Toe? • Has your teacher approved your Tic-Tac-Toe choices?	
OPTIONAL K.M.S.☺.	• Did you choose 15 or more important facts or helpful information to illustrate? • Does your rough essay show the important and interesting things you learned about your person? • Is your essay organized and easy to understand?	
IN CLASS PREP WORK	• Did you complete all activities on time? • Were you self-motivated? • Were you a good listener? • Did you follow directions independently? • Did you work hard? • Did you stay on task during class time?	
TOTAL	PREPARATION POINTS	___ = %

TEACHER PARTICIPATION OBSERVATION LOG: Students: Your teacher will be recording comments as you work independently in the classroom. You will be called up at random times for mini-conferences with your teacher. These written observations will assist your teacher in determining your final participation points.

6a Tic-Tac-Toe

#1 CREATE A GUIDEBOOK 15 FACTS	**#2** PERFORM A HUMOROUS REPORT 15 FACTS	**#3** PUBLISH A NEWSLETTER WITH 5 COLUMNS & 5 PICTURES
#4 CREATE A PHOTO ESSAY 15 FACTS	**#5** YOUR CHOICE HERE	**#6** CREATE A CHILDREN'S BOOK 15 FACTS
#7 CREATE A PUPPET SHOW 15 FACTS	**#8** CREATE A GLOGSTER 15 FACTS	**#9** DESIGN A GAME BOARD 15 FACTS

Dear students: Choose your activities in a Tic-Tac-Toe design that includes the middle square!

You will complete 3 squares – now choose!

I have selected items: #5, #_____ and #_____.

_____   _____

Student Signature   Date   Parent Signature   Date

Use the Web 2.0 and APPS handout to create electronic products!

7   Important Questions

Name _____   Date _____

PASSION LEARNING TOPIC & PERSON _____

Directions: Write two important questions for each of the words below. You will use these questions as guides as you research your passion learning person. These questions should lead you to **FACTS AND DATA** related to your person.

TYPE OF QUESTION	QUESTION #1	QUESTION #2
WHO		
WHAT		
WHERE		
WHEN		
WHY		
HOW		

8   Presentation Rubric and Fact Sheet

TASK	1 – 2 pts	3-4 pts	5-6 pts	7-8 pts	9-10 pts	Product #1	Product #2	Product #3
Presentation of Product	Mumbled Quiet	Rambled Unclear	Needed Prompting	Mostly Clear	Precise & Clear	Points /10	Points /10	Points /10
Task Commitment	Minimal Work	Basic Work	Acceptable Work	Extra Effort	Above Beyond	Points /10	Points /10	Points /10
Info or #1 Facts #2 *** #3	0-5 0-5 0-5	6-8 6-8 6-8	9-11 9-11 9-11	12-13 12-13 12-13	14-15 14-15 14-15	Points /10	Points /10	Points /10
Final Product Appearance	Inadequate or little care	Not neat	OK - needs more details	Visually appealing	Eye Catching Beyond Expectation	Points /10	Points /10	Points /10
TOTAL PTS.						/40	/40	/40

Name _____   Person_____

Product #1 _____   Total Pts. _____   Date Due _____   Date In _____

Product #2 _____   Total Pts. _____   Date Due _____   Date In _____

Product #3 _____   Total Pts. _____   Date Due _____   Date In _____

*** Facts will be evaluated as interesting, useful, and/or informative.

8	Fact Sheet for Products	
PRODUCT #1 _____ _____	PRODUCT #2 _____ _____	PRODUCT #3 _____ _____
1.	1.	1.
2.	2.	2.
3.	3.	3.
4.	4.	4.
5.	5.	5.
6.	6.	6.
7.	7.	7.
8.	8.	8.
9.	9.	9.
10.	10.	10.
11.	11.	11.
12.	12.	12.
13.	13.	13.
14.	14.	14.
15.	15.	15.

NOTE: Students: This list should be short versions of your facts for each product. I will use this list to evaluate your product as you complete each presentation. Have this form completed before you present. Good luck and I look forward to viewing your final products!

10   Teacher Planning & Organization Calendar

STAGES	MONDAY	TUESDAY	WEDNESDAY	THURSDAY	FRIDAY
1	JOURNAL I INTRO PASSION LETTER	INTRO ALPHA THINK TANK	PASSION VIDEO PART I JOURNAL II	JOURNAL III ALPHA THINK TANK WORK	ALPHA THINK TANK DUE
2	FAMOUS PEOPLE THINK TANK	FAMOUS PEOPLE THINK TANK	PASSION VIDEO PART II	FAMOUS PEOPLE THINK TANK	FAMOUS PEOPLE THINK TANK DUE
3	TWENTY-FIVE FACT CARDS	SIGNED INTRO LETTER DUE	PASSION VIDEO PART III	TWENTY-FIVE FACT CARDS	TWENTY-FIVE FACT CARDS DUE
4	TEACHER STUDENT PLANNING CONF.		PASSION VIDEO PART IV		
5	TEACHER STUDENT PROD. I CONF.		PASSION VIDEO PART V		PRODUCT II DUE
6	TEACHER STUDENT PROD. II CONF	PASSION VIDEO LOG DUE	PRODUCT I PRESENT	PRODUCT I PRESENT	PRODUCT II PRESENT
7	TEACHER STUDENT OPTIONAL CONF.				PRODUCT III DUE
8	PRODUCT II PRESENT	PRODUCT II PRESENT	PRODUCT II PRESENT	MAKE-UP PRESENT	MAKE-UP PRESENT PRODUCT III DUE
9	PRODUCT III PRESENT	PRODUCT III PRESENT	PRODUCT III PRESENT	MAKE-UP PRESENT	MAKE-UP PRESENT

NOTE: Due dates are general guidelines and may be adjusted to integrate other learning goals. Presentations are scheduled over several dates so part of each class period can be allocated for continued product work. The blank dates are for student product work sessions or for teacher needs. These stages do not have to be sequential – other instruction can be interspersed.

THE COMMON CORE STATE STANDARDS

The Common Core State Standards (CCSS) represent both a common baseline for academic knowledge and the cognitive and social skills necessary for college readiness. It is this combination that will prepare our students for the complexity of learning and living in the 21st century workforce. The Partnership for 21 Century Skills (P21) and other organizations have been advocating for this type of change that broadens the perspective of educators by challenging them to look beyond core academic skills as the desired outcome of K-college institutions. P21 puts this simply by asking education leaders to focus on fusing the rigor of the 3Rs (Core Academic Content: Reading, 'Riting, and 'Rithmetic) with the new targets of the 4 Cs:

- Critical Thinking and Problem Solving
- Communication

- Collaboration
- Creativity and Innovation

Curiosita Teaching™ is a unique and innovative program that includes the 4 Cs within its creativity framework. P21 recently released the P21 Common Core Toolkit to demonstrate how the 4 Cs are aligned to the Common Core State Standards within English Language Arts and Mathematics. To help educators understand the practical applications of creativity listed below are the CCSS references with sample student outcomes. The specific CCSS can be located using these reference numbers.

<u>CCSS</u>	<u>Sample Student Outcome (Creativity)</u>
RI.4.3 W.4.9 SL.4.1	Frame, analyze and synthesize information from a range of texts in order to solve problems and answer questions.
W.4.3 W.4.6	Develop, implement and communicate new ideas to others through original writing.
RI.8.2 RST.6-8.7 WHST.6-8.8	Use information accurately and creatively for the issue or problem at hand.
W.8.2 SL.8.2	Analyze, compare and contrast authors' and artists' motivations for creativity.
RL.11-12.9 SL.11-12.2 WHST.11-12.4 WHST.11-12.5	Students collaboratively write a proposal to help solve a community problem in innovative ways.
RH.11-12.2 W.11-12.8 SL.11-12.5	Demonstrate ability to work effectively with diverse teams.

4.MD.1 4.G.1	Students work collaboratively to "map" a box city using number sense, measurement, scale and geometry.
4.OA.3 4.NBT.6	Students use math content knowledge to understand basic concepts of financial literacy.
4.OA.2 4.OA.5 4.MD.2	Participants examine common games such as board and card games, and discuss the mathematical thinking that is involved.
8.G.1 8.G.5	Students work in teams to solve mathematical problems; they listen to the reasoning of others and offer correction with supporting arguments; they modify their own arguments when corrected; they learn from mistakes and make repeated attempts at solving problems creatively.
N-Q.1 F-LE.2 8.SP.4	Students use algebraic thinking, statistics, critical thinking and problem solving skills to compare and contrast outcomes in a sports game.
N-Q.1 N-Q.2 S-IC.3 S-IC.5	Students use creativity and innovation to compare, contrast and create algorithms to solve complex puzzles.
F-LE.1 S-CP.5	Students use statistics and probability knowledge, as well as critical thinking skills, to solve problems.

Students must have instruction in creativity (creative and critical thinking) to be able to fully participate in the sample student tasks listed above. The Curiosita Teaching Program™ provides explicit instruction to improve the creative abilities of all students.

Abbreviations for the Common Core State Standards

F-LE =	Function, Linear and Exponential	RST =	Reading Science, and Technical
G =	Geometry	S-CP =	Statistics, Conditional and Probability
MD =	Measurement and Data	S-IC =	Statistics, Inferences, and Conclusions
MD.1 =	Mathematics Measurement and Data	SL =	Speaking and Listening
NBT =	Numbers Operations Base Ten	SP =	Sequence, Series and Patterns
N-Q =	Number and Quantity	W =	Writing
OA =	Operations and Algebraic Thinking	WHST =	Writing, History, Social Studies/Science
RH -	Reading and History		and Technical
RL =	Reading Literature		

About the Authors

Patti Garrett Shade has worked in the education field for 30 years as a consultant, author, and educator. Her teaching background encompasses elementary through high school in the areas of creativity, thinking skills, and science. She taught creative thinking through a variety of middle school class offerings, including science, creative and critical thinking tools, and digital animation courses. The materials produced in this book, such as the Creative Abilities Learning Log, Creativity Introductory Scope & Sequence, and the Product-based learning Units evolved through her work in these various classroom settings. She received national recognition for both her work as a state director of gifted and talented and for the development of an elementary science lab enrichment program. She also led a successful state-wide initiative promoting both differentiation and creativity through a multi-level integrated service team. Her *work* as an educator focuses on creating interactive learning environments that result in the production of rigorous student work. She shares her learning experiences with other educators in sessions designed to offer innovative, practical, and engaging classroom instructional strategies. She is passionate about supporting educators as they respond to the differentiated needs of creative learners . . . classrooms where students have the "freedom to think!"

Dr. Rick Shade is an internationally known author, consultant, and educator. He authored ***License to Laugh: Humor in the Classroom,*** a premier book, providing educators with a new perspective on the role humor plays in the teaching and learning process. His teaching background spans primary through university in the areas of gifted and talented, special needs, creativity, and humor. As a university professor, he received "Outstanding Educator" awards at the University of Wyoming and Ball State University for innovative teaching practices. While at the University of Wyoming, he designed and delivered an annual humor and creativity summer institute for high school students. At Ball State University he created and taught a college-level *dream-course* on creativity. Rick also worked as a Senior Lecturer in the Research Center for Able Pupils at Oxford University in England. He consulted with educators throughout England and Europe providing tools, tips, and techniques designed to assist educators as they strove to improve their practice. Rick's workshops are in demand and described by participants as "fast-paced, fun, and extremely practical."

www.curiositateaching.com
info@curiositateaching.com
Curiosita Teaching Facebook